WINNING *with* HORSES

Also by

Shelley Onderdonk and *Adam Snow*
Polo Life: Horses, Sport, 10 and Zen

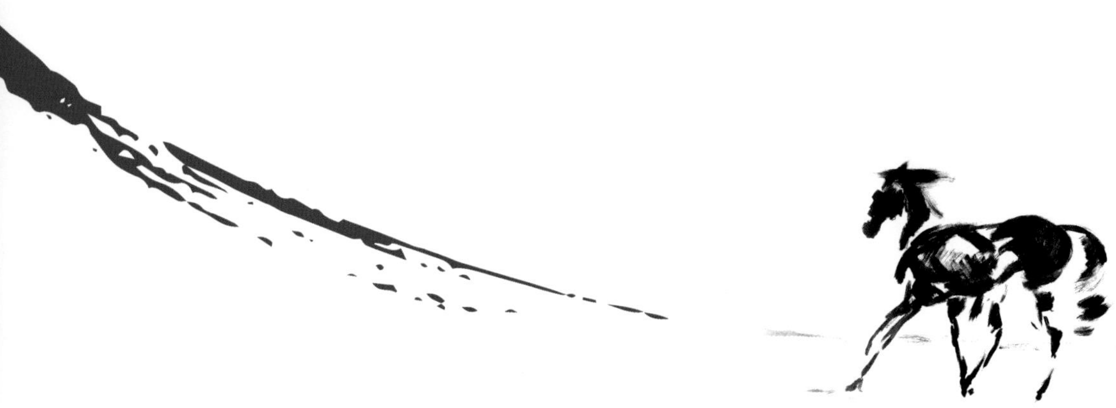

WINNING *with* HORSES

How One of the Best Polo Players of All Time
and a Sport Horse Veterinarian
Balance Human Goals with Equine Needs

Shelley Onderdonk
Adam Snow

Foreword by *Matt Brown*,
5* Event Rider

Trafalgar Square
North Pomfret, Vermont

First published in 2023 by

Trafalgar Square Books
North Pomfret, Vermont 05053

Library of Congress Cataloging-in-Publication Data
Names: Onderdonk, Shelley, author. | Snow, Adam, author.
Title: Winning with horses : how one of the best polo players of all time and a sport horse veterinarian balance human goals with equine needs / Adam Snow and Shelley Onderdonk.
Description: North Pomfret, Vermont : Trafalgar Square Books, 2023. | Summary: "Is it possible to be simultaneously passionate about winning in an equestrian sport and about the welfare of horses? Professional polo player Adam Snow and sport horse veterinarian Shelley Onderdonk answer this undeniably twenty-first-century question with a resounding, "Yes!" They have spent a lifetime together, nurturing Adam's astounding career at the top of his sport (he is the last American polo player to achieve the perfect 10-goal handicap) with the artful, conscientious care and training of the equine partners he needed to be the best. And Shelley's twenty-five years as an equine veterinarian have been spent helping sport horses compete at the highest levels in other disciplines, as well-including reining, racing, eventing, show jumping, and dressage-while always prioritizing long-term health and well-being. In these pages, Adam and Shelley share the keys to their success...and the struggles and celebrations that taught them along the way"-- Provided by publisher.
Identifiers: LCCN 2022056019 (print) | LCCN 2022056020 (ebook) | ISBN 9781646011728 (paperback) | ISBN 9781646011308 (epub)
Subjects: LCSH: Horse sports. | Horse sports injuries--Prevention. | Equine sports medicine. | Horses--Health.
Classification: LCC SF294.2 .S66 2023 (print) | LCC SF294.2 (ebook) | DDC 617.1/0278--dc23/eng/20230215
LC record available at https://lccn.loc.gov/2022056019
LC ebook record available at https://lccn.loc.gov/2022056020

All photographs ©*Robb Scharetg/Scharetgpictures.com* except: 1.1, 4.3, 6., 6.2 A & B, 7.1, 8.1, 8.2, 10.1, 10.2, 14.1, 14.2 A (*David Lominska*); 6.3 (*Snoopy Productions*); 9.1 (*Margaret Armendariz*); 12.1 A–G (*Kalie Roos*); 13.1 (*GRC Photos*); 13.2 (*Pam Gleason*); 2.1, 14.2 B (courtesy of *Adam Snow*); 2.2, 11.1 (courtesy of *Shelley Onderdonk*)
Illustrations by *Kate Mieczkowska*
Book design by *Katarzyna Misiukanis-Celińska (https://misiukanis-artstudio.com)*
Cover design by *RM Didier*
Typefaces: *Miller Text*, *Metropolis* and *Timberline*
Index by *Andrea M. Jones (www.jonesliteraryservice.com)*

Printed in China
10 9 8 7 6 5 4 3 2 1

To the horses, who have been
our greatest teachers of all.

// Contents

// Foreword

Foreword

When Shelley Onderdonk asked me to write the foreword to the book she was writing with her husband, Adam Snow, I felt honored and more than a little amazed she and Adam would ask me. My wife Cecily and I have written some blogs and articles related to horse sports over the years, but writing a foreword for a book—and not just *any* book, but a book written by two people we have so much respect and love for—felt a little daunting. Shelley told me about the premise of the book and emailed me the manuscript so I could read it and decide if I wanted to write the foreword. Of course, before even reading the book, I was super excited to be involved, not only because Adam and Shelley have had a fascinating journey with horses and in creating the team that would make Adam one of the greatest American polo players of all time, but also because over the last few years we've had so many wonderful conversations with them about horses, horse people (we are an odd bunch), and the joy and uncertainty of competing with horses.

Cecily and I grew up riding and competing in Northern California—she was in the hunter-jumper world and I was an event rider. A shared love and passion for horses brought us together, and our commitment to their well-being and our own development as trainers and competitors have driven our goals and dreams since.

In 2015, after building a successful horse training business on the West Coast, we made the difficult decision to uproot in our quest to realize my Olympic dream and ended up trading the golden hills of California for the lush green landscape of Southeastern Pennsylvania. We moved to an area of the country steeped in a long tradition of riding, including fox hunting, timber racing, polo, and eventing. Our new home base was the perfect setting for reestablishing our business and for me to continue my competitive career.

In the late summer of 2015, we were in the process of finding a winter location for our eventing competition business when we met Shelley and Adam. It was the first time we would be "migrating" south, along with the rest of the shivering and frostbitten northeastern horse crowd, to spend the winter months in a more hospitable climate for training horses. Aiken, South Carolina, with its thriving horse community representing all sorts of different equine-related sports and activities, seemed like the perfect place for us to escape the snow and mud of a Pennsylvania winter. (Horse people trying to work and ride outside in Pennsylvania in the winter have the same appreciation for mud that a horse has for horseflies.)

We were put in contact with Adam by Deirdre Stoker Vaillancourt, an endlessly connected Aiken realtor and rider (and oh, by the way, her husband was a Grand Prix jumper rider and is still a top-level show jumping course designer and clinician, which just goes to show how Aiken is a bastion of horse enthusiasts). The only thing we knew about Adam and Shelley was that they had a beautiful horse property and had stalls to rent for the winter.

Driving down their winding drive for the first time, we fell in love. We could see big green pastures with groups of happy polo ponies, beautifully maintained practice polo fields, and a fairly humble pole barn amid the setting of Aiken horse country. As we pulled up to the barn to meet Adam and finalize our winter plans, I saw him dismounting and I thought to myself, "Oh, that's cool—he rides!" Being a male in a sport dominated by women, I'm always kind of surprised when I see other men who ride.

We had been on the property with all our horses and clients for several weeks before I found out Adam was a really good polo player...and it was probably several more weeks before I learned he was one of America's greatest players of all time! You see, Adam is the kind of horseman who watches and asks questions more than he espouses his own expertise. He was always interested in how we were training our own horses or how we prepared them for competition. He often asked about some piece of equipment we were using or what we thought of some training technique.

When we finally got to see him ride, it was like watching a tennis ball floating in the ocean, going in and out with the tide. There was a calmness to it. A flow. He could be chasing down the ball with his mallet raised, but he always looked relaxed and was always with his horse. In the barn, I also noticed how Adam always spent time with his horses. Whether he was grooming them, working with one of his homebreds in the round pen, or out on a hack, it was clear he loved them.

We didn't meet Shelley until after we moved to the property. We were first struck by her vibrant energy, and similar to Adam, her humble nature. She maintained a busy vet practice but was around the barn a lot working with her own horses as well as the polo ponies. We saw her doing everything from normal vet care to acupuncture and bodywork to trimming feet. Sometimes she would be in the round pen with a young horse or out doing some dressage and jumping in one of the practice fields.

It was easy to see how much knowledge she had, and before too long, we were asking her advice on the vet care and management of our own horses. She also started doing acupuncture and bodywork on our horses, which turned out to be invaluable, because not only did the horses feel good after she worked on them, but she would always have insights into the horses muscling and recommendations for exercises that could help the horses' development.

After spending a few years wintering at their property, Cecily and I grew to have a huge appreciation for Adam and Shelley—how they worked together, how their horses and ours were content and happy, and how their love and care for the horses drove what they did each day. They have been able to develop partnerships with their horses, not only where the horses are happy in their work but also well-trained enough and confident enough to compete at the highest level of sport.

Their book *Winning with Horses* isn't so much of a manual of training and techniques, rather it's two incredible horsemen sharing their experiences from a lifetime with horses. It reminds us to observe and listen to our horses, to listen to the advice of our mentors, and to listen to our own gut and instinct. Like one of my favorite books on horses, *Horses Never Lie* by Mark Rashid, this book helps us understand how we should *think* about training horses, how we should approach *our philosophy* in training horses. Because there are a million different techniques that can be used to train a horse, but if the reason behind what you're doing isn't there, then it will never be successful. Technique is nothing without philosophy.

Since moving East, I have been lucky enough to have been a part of high-performance equestrian sport as member of US Nations Cup teams for eventing in Aachen, Germany, and Boekelo, Netherlands, as well as reserve rider for the US Eventing Team at the 2016 Olympics in Rio de Janeiro and for the 2015 Pan American Games in Toronto. I have witnessed the heights to which a true partnership with horses can take a person, and unfortunately, I've also witnessed the fragility of that partnership when a competitor reaches toward those heights without regard for a horse's health or longevity. It is easy to become jaded and to see only one of two options: either be competitive, and in doing so, make decisions that will likely jeopardize the health of the horse or his longevity; *or* value the horse to the detriment of competitive results. In *Winning with Horses*, Adam and Shelley show us *there is a way to do both*, and in these pages, they tell us how they found that way.

One of the many ways Adam and Shelley describe accomplishing competitive success while still honoring the horse that really resonated with me is the idea of having separate roles as "the competitor" and "the horse advocate." As Adam describes, as "the competitor," we can only play "free" if we are free of worry—of the outcome or result and of the condition of the horse. It is so easy to let competitive goals cloud our judgment.

"The horse advocate" should be your trusted advisor who knows the horse and has a thorough understanding of the horse's physical and mental strengths and weaknesses, and who takes on the role of making sure the horse is healthy and ready to compete. In this scenario "the competitor" is free to focus on the competition because decisions related to the horse's well-being, long-term health, and whether the horse should or shouldn't compete are in the hands of "the horse advocate."

One of the goals of this book is to help us learn there is no performance without trust and to help us with strategies so we can "consciously compete" in partnership with our horses. We won't always make the right calls, but with the right philosophy behind our training and with the goal of keeping the horse first in our decisions, it *is* possible to win with horses while respecting them at the same time. This book shows that these two ideas are not mutually exclusive.

For me, *Winning with Horses* has become a reference guide, a signpost, helping me navigate my own competitive goals and my horses' health and happiness. In the modern landscape of horse sports and society's increasingly fragile acceptance of the use of horses in sport, as well as the revelations made in the last decade in the areas of our understanding of horse behavior and physiology and in human sports psychology, it is the modern horsemen's guide we *all* need. Every person's competitive career with horses should start with this book. //

Matt Brown, 5* Event Rider
East West Training Stables, Kennett Square, Pennsylvania

CHAPTER

1

An Introduction

A horse! A horse!
My kingdom for a horse!

Richard III,
– William Shakespeare –

// An Introduction

In the spring of 1986, Adam Snow introduced himself to me in Yale's Payne Whitney Gymnasium. For our second date, we drove down the Merritt Parkway to watch the Cup of the Americas polo match between North America and Argentina. He was surprised I had agreed to join. Granted, the game featured the best players in the world but Adam assumed, correctly, that I knew nothing about polo and therefore saw it as a portent for how smitten I was after the meal and drinks we had shared on our first date at Viva Zapata's in New Haven, Connecticut. Later, he understood things more clearly—I was going to watch the horses.

On June 3, 1989, Adam and I were married. And, though we have lived in many places around the world, since 1992 we have called Aiken, South Carolina, our home. It is here that we have raised our three sons, and nurtured the farm (named New Haven Farm after the city where we met) and the many horses with which you will soon be familiar.

Out of college Adam was not sure about his career path, and so he found his way to Argentina with the vague intention of learning Spanish and

CHAPTER 1

/ 1.1 / Amy won the Best Playing Pony prize in the 2009 US Open. She was exceptional because she was inexhaustible and always gave Adam the two options—run or stop—that he needed to control the game.

improving his polo. His goal was to get to play one season professionally in Florida. Once in Buenos Aires, he found a working internship on a breeding and training *estancia,* which resulted in a contract to play the 1988 winter season in Palm Beach, Florida. This exposure brought a cascade of playing opportunities. Over the next several decades Adam worked his way up via talent, ambition, and perseverance to win more and more tournaments at increasingly higher levels. In 2003 he made it to the top of the sport, achieving a perfect 10-goal handicap (at the time of this writing, he is the last American player to have been raised to 10 goals).

Adam couldn't have made it to 10 goals without his equine partners—he had a reputation of owning great horses who were impeccably maintained. And though I sometimes lamented the fact that our own partnership leaned heavily toward supporting his successful career, I took pride in my contribution to the lives of these amazing animals. Adam and I soaked up the wisdom of more experienced horse people, added our own intuitions, and poured our combined effort (mental as well as physical) into these horses. Training them and maintaining them became an obsession. Their proficiency propelled Adam's teams to tournament wins; and their Best Playing Pony awards (forty-four to be precise!) brought validation that our "secret sauce" was working. Amy, Muffin, Baby Doll, Mirage, Hoorah, Tequila... each time that coveted "BPP" blanket adorned one of these equine athletes, it bestowed recognition on our entire New Haven Farm team.

As for me, from the time I read James Herriot's books (*All Creatures Great and Small* is the best-known) as a child, I knew that I wanted to be a veterinarian. In college I joked I was an "in-the-closet, pre-vet student" (I was surrounded by more ambitious folk going to medical school or MD-PhD programs). I graduated from the University of Georgia veterinary school in 1987. In 1998 I started my certification training in veterinary acupuncture, and soon thereafter opened my own equine veterinary practice. I was juggling a lot between my job and motherhood and managing Adam's horse program, but I was in my element and loved all the different hats I wore. My innate nerdiness has propelled me to always want to be learning—I have continued to further my education, taking courses in *Tui Na* (a traditional form of Chinese manual therapy or "soft" chiropractic), pain management, herbal medicine, nutrition, and sports medicine. I particularly love the part of my veterinary work where I am trying to figure out the last piece of the jigsaw puzzle that allows a horse's performance to rise from 90 to 100 percent. I have focused the majority of my 25-year career as an equine veterinarian on helping sport horses to compete at the highest levels in disciplines that range from reining to racing, eventing to dressage, and jumping to polo, while always prioritizing long-term health.

In 2016 Adam and I published our first book, *Polo Life: Horses, Sport, 10 & Zen,* which detailed our lives in the sport of polo. There was a question percolating in those

pages that intrigued many readers—namely, is it possible to be simultaneously passionate about winning *and* about horses? Our answer is a resounding *yes*. And this book is devoted to that idea. We describe what steps horse people must take to compete, and win, in sport while at the same time being conscientious stewards of horses' welfare.

Some of the subjects we explore are:

/ **1** / What considerations does a competitor have to keep in mind to effectively balance short-term goals with longevity in a chosen discipline? This often comes down to making strategic training and veterinary decisions.

/ **2** / Does innovation in the horse industry drive improvements in horse welfare or are horses better served by keeping horse care natural? You'll see how we strive to embrace new ideas without losing our common sense. Our evaluation for balancing the natural with the innovative recognizes that "unnatural" interventions—tack, shoes, and grain—have to be utilized in a manner commensurate with the questions being asked of the equestrian athletes, while not disrupting the patterns established over millions of years of evolution.

/ **3** / Since resources of money and knowledge are finite, how does one decide what to prioritize and which goals to streamline? We hope to describe easy ways to evaluate and not become stymied by the inevitable onslaught of information. In the opportunistic horse world of people trying to push (and sell) their latest fad, we tack towards simplicity. One way to simplify: focus on making your competition horses athletes, not supermodels.

The ethics of equestrian sport are complicated. Adam and I have chosen to write this book as a team precisely because of the distinct perspective we each bring. In these pages we alternate control of the narrative, with the polo player avatar representing Adam's voice, and the running horse figure seen at the beginning of this Introduction mine. Our disparate vantage points illustrate the existence of multiple paths to the same destination, where we firmly agree that it is entirely possible to be both ambitious and compassionate. Our goal: give the horse every chance to be his best.

Adam's mentor once told him that in high-goal polo the quality of a team's horses accounts for up to 80 percent of a team's success. I'd be willing to bet that this would be a similar valuation for most other elite equine sports—for example, in the Olympic selection process it is primarily the horse that gets chosen, not the rider. Perhaps this is because there are many riders who work hard, are highly accomplished, and are experienced competitors, so it is the horse at the end of the day that has to have that ineffable "something" to make the supreme athletic effort that brings about a chance to win.

But there is also the partnership part of the equation. An integral part of winning in equestrian sports centers around humans' ability to foster positive equine relationships. At some point when times are tough, your horse will have a choice of whether to do what is asked of him. And if there is a reservoir of good feeling, the answer is more likely to be "yes." If you can always ask yourself in your interactions with your horse, "What does my horse need from me as a caretaker, as a rider, as a trainer, and as a competitor?" then you are on the road to benefitting from a wondrous relationship. You can learn how to navigate that fine line between wanting to get the most from your horse without taking anything away.

Our story is an explicit acknowledgment that doing good for the horse is good for results in the competitive arena. Our task is to explain our method, and yours is to prove that it can be replicated. We hope anyone—from the first-time rider learning the ropes to a successful professional looking for that 1 percent difference that will put them on top—will find our discussions useful. Although we are not experts in every field and do not pretend this is a how-to manual, we offer our stories, our experiences, and the accumulated wisdom from countless hours of learning from those more knowledgeable than ourselves. We want to pass it on—how to win for yourself, and win for your horse.

Although we may not depend on the horse for survival, as King Richard allegedly did on the battlefield all those years ago, we agree with the sentiment: *it's always been about the horse*. Here's what we've learned through them, because of them, with them. Our learning is ongoing. //

end *of* chapter 1

CHAPTER

2

Why Horses?

All roads lead to horses.

// Why Horses?

Adam's Take: The Ball Came First

My own earliest associations with horses are of family pressure to get on one. Occasionally, my dad would persuade me to help him "exercise the ponies." This occurred on trails through the woods near our home in Hamilton, Massachusetts. On cold mornings, the animals' breath appeared like puffs of smoke being emitted from fire-breathing nostrils. I would clench the reins tight and follow as closely as possible the tail of the horse in front me. This, I felt at the time, was the safest spot.

At some stage my grandfather, who I knew as "Too," a career pilot, put a mallet in my hand, offered up his steady gelding, B-Fly, and directed me to "swing through the ball" (white and wooden).

"Let your follow-through *fly* in the direction you want the ball to travel," Too instructed.

But it wasn't until that ball actually got bowled in to commence play—and I was competing alongside peers of a similar age (my younger brother,

CHAPTER

2

/ 2.1 / Adam on Quince in one of his first games.

Andrew, among them)—that I threw caution to the wind and began to ride, and play, with abandon. I was 12 years old, and all in. There were goals to be scored, plays to be devised (with Andrew back at the barn as we cleaned tack), and communication with another species to improve in order to get to the ball first. The last became an ongoing quest.

But, if horses once represented just a means of getting to the ball, this changed when I began to own, train, and play my own polo ponies. At this stage, I began to focus on (and enjoy) the "equestrian side" of the sport of polo as much or more than the "ball side." The horses became central, not only to getting to the ball first, but to my life with Shelley.

This transition was phased. For several years, I had enjoyed traveling around the world with only my boots and mallets to worry about. But the situation was not sustainable. The sharp curve of improvement I had enjoyed straight out of college was sure to flatten. And the higher my handicap rose, the better the horses I required to play well on that rating. I could foresee the day when the quality of horses I was being loaned would become the limiting factor to my improvement.

One 10-goal mentor, Alfonso Pieres, told me, "It's hard to play bad on a good horse." As my handicap rose and the competition became more elite, I realized that the converse of this equation could also be true.

In August of 1991, Shelley and I visited Sheridan, Wyoming, and bought two three-year-old Thoroughbreds—Kansas and Darwin—from Mimi and Bob Tate. That fall in Wellington, Florida, where Shelley was working as a veterinary technician, we secured two stalls and rode Kansas and Darwin together every

★ Polo 101

For those unfamiliar with the sport of polo, here are some of the basics, which will be referred to in the pages ahead.

Polo is played four versus four horse-and-rider pairs and is often described as "hockey on horseback." One big difference, however, is that the size of a polo field—300 yards by 160 yards or 10 acres—is massive in comparison with a rink or even a football field. In fact, 10 football fields fit into the area of one polo field.

Fundamental to the game is its handicap system whereby each player is designated a rating of "-1" to "10." The sum of the four teammates' "goal ratings" determines the team's total handicap. Tournaments have set handicap limits and are hosted by clubs or the national governing body. Currently the US Open, for example, is played at the maximum limit of 22 goals.

The vast majority of professional polo players are from Argentina, which dominates in almost every demographic of the sport. But there are also world-class players from England, Spain, South Africa, Uruguay, and the United States. Matches are typically six, seven-and-a-half-minute periods, called chukkers. Total duration—with stoppages, a half-time "divot stomp" for spectators to put the field back, and breaks to change horses—is, on average, a little under two hours.

People unfamiliar with the sport are often surprised by the numbers of "ponies" that participate in a single match. (We use the expression "pony," but they are really horses, mostly Thoroughbreds, and usually between 15 to 16 hands tall.) I played six ponies in the finals of the 2002 US Open, and this was the shortest list I had played during the entire season. For most matches, I brought a string of nine, and usually ended up playing eight of these. The one that did not play, I used to warm-up on ("stick and ball") before the match. Today's high-goal (high-handicap) players, who usually also have the most depth in horses, may play up to a dozen horses in a single match, "splitting chukkers" whenever possible, in order to always be riding a fresh pony. These mid-chukker changes can either be made "on-the-fly," like a line change in ice hockey, or during a break in play, like immediately after a goal is scored or when a referee blows the whistle for a foul. ▶

Polo balls have evolved from willow root to today's plastic, are slightly larger than a baseball, and are hard but light. Goals may be scored at any height through the two goal posts, which are separated by 24 feet and stand at either end of the field. A "long hit" would be considered anything over 100 yards. And the longest goals are scored from around midfield, 150 yards out; however, the majority of goals are scored by tapping it through the goalposts on breakaways or from the 30-, 40- and 60-yard penalty lines. A typical final score would be in the range of 12 goals to 10.

The rules are based on the line of the ball and are loosely comparable to the rules of the road when driving in the United Kingdom or a former colony. One can meet oncoming traffic keeping the line of the ball, or median, on your right—for this reason, all players must carry the mallet in their right hand—but cannot cross over this right of way at a distance perceived to be dangerous. "Hooking" (when a player uses his mallet to block or interfere with an opponent's swing) is allowed on the same side of the horse as the player with the ball, as long as it is below the shoulder; and "bumps" or "ride-offs" (when one player pushes against an opponent in an effort to move him off the line of the ball or to stop him from receiving the ball) are allowed with a similar speed and safe degree of angle. These are the bare basics, and all polo rules are intended to protect the safety of horse and rider. Two mounted officials with whistles patrol the field as referees, and a third official sits in the stands in case a tie-breaking vote becomes necessary.

Our focus in these pages is competing with horses in any equestrian sport while keeping the horses' interests clearly in mind. For this reason, I intentionally do not make a deep dive into the sport of polo. It is my hope that the context will provide some understanding, even for those readers who have never seen a polo match. But the emphasis is intended to be on the horse, and ultimately, the discipline itself matters little. **//**

morning, training them for better rides and future competitions. They were the first two horses either of us had ever owned.

The pursuit of finding and training our own horses soon took on a life of its own. Because we couldn't afford top playing horses, the process of getting mounted required ingenuity, the recognition of untapped talent, and then a plan to nurture and train that prospect to its full potential. Shelley's help—namely her eye, and her skills on the back of young horses—was critical to this process. Incrementally, season by season, we continued buying horses until I realized that the horses—finding, training, maintaining, and playing the best ponies I could afford—had become my passion. There were stages to this evolution, many mistakes, and (hopefully) a progression of learning. I think horses are great teachers, and humility is certainly one of their primary lessons.

One year I was invited to a Buck Brannaman clinic at a friend's farm in Memphis, Tennessee. It was essentially my introduction to what had come to be known as "natural horsemanship." My eyes were opened to a new way of thinking, and a new range of training and communication skills to try with our own horses. "Make the wrong thing difficult, and the right thing easy," Buck's mentor, Ray Hunt, had said. During this time Shelley became a veterinarian and contributed with every ounce of her brains, bravery (she always rode the youngest horses before me), equitation, and professional expertise. When our horse Muffin won the Best Playing Pony prize in 1997 for the East Coast Open, the first such honor for one of our own horses, it felt like the proudest moment of my career, even though my team had lost the game.

So, gradually, inevitably, the horses themselves—my consistent *teammates*—had become the beating heart of my polo life.

As a child, I had begun by chasing a ball on horseback. Soon I realized that effective communication with my horse was the way to be first to that ball. To this day, working on that communication continues to be an endless—and enjoyable—process. //

end *of* adam's part

Shelley's Take: Some Are Born That Way

There is a photograph of me from the summer of 1999 in Montana where my smile is as broad as the blue sky above me. The reason for my beaming? *I was on a horse.* I hadn't ridden much recently at that point as I had just had my second child, and being back astride gave me so much joy. Adam remarked upon seeing the photo, "Wow, I guess we sure know how to make Shelley happy."

Years before, my father had sometimes exclaimed, "There's a horse!" while hurtling down the highway at 70 miles per hour in our Ford "woody" station wagon. I'd snap to attention (no seat belt constrained me in those days) and whip my head in the direction of his finger and gaze, enraptured, where a lone horse in a roadside field was rapidly disappearing from view. I was, in the parlance, "horse crazy." I played with my Breyer® horses, and built barns and sewed blankets for them. I pretended I was a horse at recess, complete with moving on all fours and neighing, for an extended period of time in the fourth grade with a similarly besotted friend. (Maybe she was my only friend at that point.)

”
It’s almost my
favorite moment
of the day—leading
horses into the barn
for their breakfast
while witnessing
the sun rise.

/ 2.2 / On my aunt's horse, Prince, the first horse I ever rode, at my favorite place to be—my grandparents' cattle ranch in central California.

Despite some early experiences of being bucked off by a young colt or my lesson pony being naughty or falling over a jump, I had no fear of horses, and nothing they did ever intimidated me. It didn't matter that my parents weren't "horsey" or horseback riders. It didn't matter that I had to wait until I was 25 years old to have my first horse. Nothing dampened my enthusiasm. And when at 26 years old I was living in a barn, attending veterinary school, and married to a professional horseman, my family finally shrugged and conceded, "I guess it isn't a phase." Decades later, being with and around horses is still my happy place.

Sometimes I am too busy to bury my nose in my horse's neck and take a deep inhale—but each and every time I do, I am transported. When I enter into a horse's space to try and help him, I am lost to other concerns, finding flow in a beautiful dance of questions and answers. Call me an Anglophile, but I sure do hope to be riding in my nineties like Queen Elizabeth did!

Horses simply get under your skin. Perhaps one day scientists will find a gene—it feels as innate as that. And if horses are your vocation, the prospects for retirement aren't good. It is joked that polo players will "go down swinging" due to their propensity for using their last penny to finance their passion. Leading an equestrian-centered life is addictive. I can't rationally explain why in my late middle age I still prefer doing almost anything on or around a horse—*even shoveling manure*—to doing almost anything else.

Sitting astride a horse may be, like staring into a crackling campfire, a deeply atavistic pleasure. It is a feeling of power. It is a feeling of freedom. Most teenagers eagerly await the arrival of a driver's license and car keys as the ticket to independence; my teenage years were full of dreams of galloping a horse, bareback, across wide-open mountain meadows and along ridgelines. The feeling is captured in this way about a character in Deborah Levy's book *Real Estate*:

> *Agnes had a sense of her own purpose in life, which is sometimes called agency or holding the reins of the high horse and steering it. After all, there is no point in climbing onto the high horse if you don't know how to ride it.*

If you are reading this book right now, you have probably experienced at least a glimmer of these sentiments.

Sitting around a dinner table talking *about* horses can stretch for hours. Endless chatter about horse-and-rider shenanigans rolls on heedlessly, in waves of joyous heckling and nods of assent (except for those without the "gene," who will invariably slip off, wondering what all the fuss is about). But talking *with* horses, well, that rises to another level of intensity of experience. It has become my passion to understand horses to the best of my ability, during this short time I have here on Earth, sharing it with the magnificent species, the horse. I have been fortunate to have some brilliant teachers help me create the shared language between two species as epitomized by ridden classical horsemanship, and others help me learn the roots of equine language as proffered by natural horsemanship. The feeling of communicating non-verbally, whichever way it is presented, to me is transcendent. And keeps me going day after day.

As long as I am able, I wish to continue my work as a veterinarian, live on our horse farm, and keep riding. As I sit and write this, I can see my and Adam's horses spread out in various large pastures contentedly grazing. Our horses and farm have us rooted to a life in rhythm with nature, and it is a good choice for me. //

end *of* shelley's part

CHAPTER

3

Keeping Training Natural

Every time you ride your horse you are either training him or untraining him.

– George H. Morris –

// Keeping Training Natural

Those who strive to be their horse's best stewards need to ask themselves, and answer honestly, what is natural about what we are asking them to do and what is not. For example, if a horse is being asked to execute things he would naturally do in a field, like run, stop, and turn, then the goal is to preserve the innate movement, slip a rider on his back, and simply switch control from the horse brain to the human brain. When a horse is being asked to execute things that you may not witness when he is cavorting in the pasture, then some accommodations in training and tools need to be made. Every decision you make as a trainer is informed by the determination of how much intervention is appropriate. How much do you want to affect the horse's natural inclinations in when and how he moves?

To me the essence of good training is to build a reservoir of trust between horse and rider that either one can tap into when the inevitable difficulties arise.

The horse asks: *Do you really want me to go there/jump that/not be afraid of this?* And the rider responds: *Yes, I will keep you safe.*

CHAPTER 3

”

Some people talk to animals. Not many people listen though. That's the problem.

AA MILNE

Or maybe the rider observes: *There may be a spooky deer/muddy footing/ long way to travel.* And the horse responds: *Don't worry, I will keep you safe.*

A successful partnership rests on a solid foundation of communicating wisely.

Communication

Historically, human interaction with horses was based on *us* teaching *them* a new shared language based on touch (for example the riding aids that constituted classical horsemanship). Modern equestrians owe a debt to wildlife biologists such as Jane Goodall who pioneered the observation of animals in the wild as a valid scientific undertaking—in this century, observation of herd dynamics and social communication in wild horses

★ Always Your "A Game"

Horses can learn the things you don't want them to know as quickly as they learn what you want them to—and most often they are easy learners and hard un-learners. This creates a sense of purpose inherent in every interaction between you and your horse. In a wonderful way, it makes you want to bring your A Game. //

★ On Animal Communication

There are people I respect who believe in "animal communicators" (defined as people who sense and can put into English what a horse or dog may want to "say"). Although I personally don't have any proof of this happening, I also cannot disprove that someone may have that ability. What I know though, deep in my bones, is that horses understand *intention*. Around horses, you have to be very careful with your intentions. They may come true. //

jump-started the awareness that *we* can learn *their* language of body movement communication. Taking the time to teach our bodies to speak equine language enriches our shared experience. Exploring the ways your horse can "talk" to you will enable you to get the most from your horse. Learning the language of the horse is the best way to "keep it natural."

There is a third way to communicate with horses—in English (or whatever language you choose). Horses have a limited ability to discern the spoken word, however, so even the "smartest" (in human terms of intelligence) don't possess a very large vocabulary. There probably will never be a horse like the famous Border Collie Chaser, who it is said mastered the meaning of 1,022 nouns. But it still can be very satisfying to teach your horse to appropriately respond to a few words. I have taught one of my horses to understand "Whoa," "Let's go," and "Steady." All verbs and very useful under saddle. He also for a while had a misunderstanding of the meaning of "Good boy"—he thought it meant he got to stop cantering. I had to reprogram my rewards after that realization! (I swear my other horse ignores me except when I say the word "carrot.")

Training Methods

There are many ways to train a horse. In the summer of 1993, I visited the *Musée du Cheval* (The Museum of the Horse) in the Loire Valley, France. Although there were many inspiring exhibits, the galleries also chronicled a history of training horses based on the horse's desire to avoid pain.

Endless rows of harsh bits, knife-edged spurs, and snaky whips—instruments of torture. Nowadays, such methods would be considered cruel. But it is naïve to think they have completely disappeared.

Old-school "cowboy" methods of inducing equine compliance to human demands include snubbing (usually to a post or to another horse if you have an experienced cow horse available to be your helper) or tying up a front foot for immobilization. At the other end of the training methods spectrum are the modern-day "horse whisperers." They also want to teach the horse to yield to pressure, but generally take more time and use the horse's own instincts to work in their favor, rather than using force as a tool. The softest approach of these can result in a horse who responds to a human's pointed finger or turned shoulder—even a gaze.

All types of successful horse training involving a "yield" of some sort to pressure of some type and level have to do with the human part of the equation. To be successful, we need to alternate between pressure and release with a proper sense of timing and level of insistence. This, in equestrian circles, is often called "feel." How do you know how much pressure to exert? When riding, you have to feel it in your body; when doing groundwork, you have to see it through your eyes. How much pressure to exert is never "known"—it is a skill that is in continual development. Because although some elements are universal there will always be variations from horse to horse, and from day to day. Which is why the process of training is endlessly fascinating.

★ Never One Way

What I know to be true? Every horse has a slightly different answer to the same question. People like to think there is a "right" way to do something, but with horses, it seems to me that there is never one right way for every horse in every situation and with every rider. *Individualization* is the right answer, and this is where horsemanship is not a science but an art. //

★ Increase Pressure Wisely

A client of mine recently relayed a harrowing story she had witnessed: A young trainer was riding a horse with draw reins, and the horse flipped over backward and had to be put down. In my client's estimation, the horse didn't understand how to yield to pressure and the trainer didn't understand how to apply it, with tragic consequences.

There exists a plethora of written words about "training scales," and how to advance through sequential steps in order to achieve progressive goals. Those details are beyond the scope of this book but suffice it to say that all regimens are in essence a method of increasing pressure wisely. That is the take-home message when it comes to horse training, whatever your discipline: *increase pressure wisely.* Insist politely without being detrimental to the training process, or the safety of you or your horse. //

If you demand too much, a horse will feel overwhelmed and lose trust in the process. Your horse may "quit on you" or develop physical problems (such as gastric ulcers) or behavioral problems (like rearing). But if you don't ask for enough, your horse may not improve or may take advantage of you. Discipline is crucial because horses are large animals capable of doing immense harm to a human. And most of them naturally like to be bossy—it is how they function in a herd. But pushiness in a horse when a human body is involved is non-negotiable. Most horses, if you catch them young enough, learn this lesson readily. Ideally, their dams taught them to yield in their foalhood, and you can just assume the mantle of maternal authority.

The Push/Pull Dance

I wrote *cultivate the quiet but don't be afraid to discipline the dangerous* on our tack room quick-erase board when Adam was backing our two-year-old homebred, LolliBopp. This was his first experience being responsible for one of our "babies" on his own. LolliBopp was bred to the nines for polo and had an attitude to match. A naturally balanced and efficient mover, she was one of those who you knew if you got the mental part of training correct, she'd make a polo pony. She was also a gray. (Do you know any grays who get special attention?) Perhaps she got treated a little too much like a princess in her youth.

When I wrote that phrase on the board, I was thinking about the concept

/ **3.1** / LolliBopp, coming in from a practice session, all ears, eyes, and attitude.

of alternating between *following* and *yielding*, which is basic to my theory of starting a horse. *Following* means that you get the horse interested enough in you to literally follow you if you walk away, and that he comes to you willingly when asked, or in the industry parlance, that he is "joined-up." *Yielding* means that he can be directed and will go away from the pressure you exert. A correct yield will move whichever horse body part you want moved with the alacrity you desire. Dancing fluidly between the two—following and yielding—is my goal in the round pen. I want to create a place where respect and affection create a bond between two creatures.

Adam was very successful at getting LolliBopp to follow; she followed him around like a dog and was super curious and connected to him. She didn't, however, like being directed and thus yielding was sometimes a problem. Adam asked me to help a few times—he wanted me to play the "bad cop" and put enough pressure on her to make her obey (and to

"

It's our job as riders to create a situation that is simplistic to the horses. They like it simple, but it requires a very complex skill set to communicate simply. It requires, among other things, a huge amount of body control and a lack of negative emotions.

KAREN O'CONNOR,
GOLD-MEDAL-WINNING OLYMPIAN IN EVENTING

put an end to some potentially menacing dominant behaviors). And let me tell you, she always let me know how displeased she was with someone actually telling her what to do. She would toss her head and move her front feet—*high*. Kicking and bucking were favorite ploys. I didn't want to take the spunk away, so I just gradually had to teach her what was acceptable and what was not. But I wanted to make sure that her antics never got to the point of being dangerous. We still have to make that line explicit for her at times.

I happened to be in the barn when LolliBopp walked off the polo field and back into the barn after one of her first fast chukkers, and the look on her face was priceless. It basically said, *Wow. That was hard.* She was a little humbled, and was really well-behaved and quiet in the barn for a few days after that!

With most horses "cultivating the quiet" is the harder thing to accomplish, partly because they have evolved through millennia as a prey animal (about which there is not a whole lot we can do), and partly because horses can read humans like a book (about which we do have a lot of control). Whether you like it or not, your horse is often a mirror of your brain. Have you ever tried standing near your horse quietly, placing a hand on him, and taking a slow deliberate breath? You immediately make an impact on him. Thus, you *do* have to start with yourself—bring your best, calm, in-the-flow brain to every session with your horse and your chances of having a peaceful ride increase dramatically.

There are certainly differences between horses in their attitudes, some based on their prior experiences and some undoubtedly innate. But horses' willingness to trust and react responsibly is eminently moldable; I have encountered very few horses who are intractable.

★ Work on It Every Moment

People say to me, "Oh your horse is so quiet," and the subtext is always that he is just innately that way. And although there is something to that, and I say thank you politely, I often inwardly object: *You have no idea how hard it has been to get to this place! I still work on it every moment I am with my horse.*

It is worth saying again: calm is always the first priority. And that doesn't mean that it is always 100 percent achievable! It is just a goal. //

★ Tuned In

Three indications that your horse is a ready and willing partner:

1. Eye softens

2. Audibly exhales

3. Head lowers

In all your interactions, and decisions, make it foremost in your mind to exude calm. It can be challenging when we are in a rush, or stressed, or nervous. But practicing bringing out the quiet in your horse will also rebound and help you become less rushed, less stressed, and less nervous. For your safety, for your horse's safety, and for everyone's enjoyment and success, a quiet horse is the goal. There is also the crucial benefit that when a crisis does truly occur, a positive outcome is more likely.

Riding Patterns

Being a little bit of a math geek, I often think about my rides in terms of geometry. I learned years ago from an instructor that you can allow the shape you are riding to dictate the balance and speed of your horse. Just ride the line—whether it be a barrel-racing cloverleaf, circle,

/ 3.2 A–D / In training, let the horse be frisky. Let him be free; let him find his own balance and self-carriage. It's a pact: mutual respect; mutual care. Take the time to check in, rest, "cultivate the quiet" **(A)**. Practice following on a long loose rope **(B)**. Encourage your horse to find self-carriage on the rope **(C)**. Using body cues, you can then help your horse find self-carriage at liberty **(D)**.

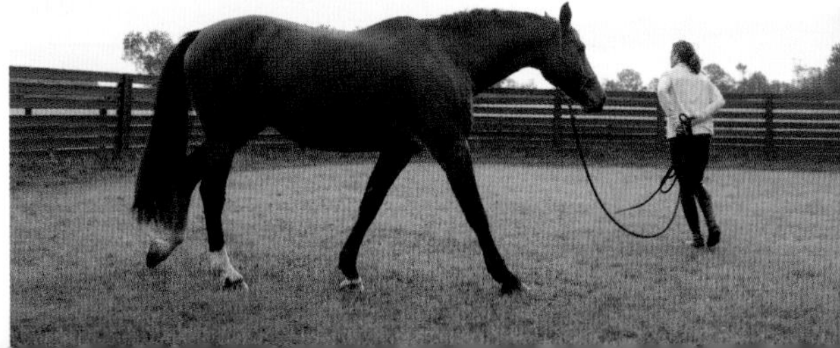

★ The Ditch Test

We have a small drainage ditch along one side of a field on our farm that I love to use. When I think a horse is ready, I'll see if he passes my "ditch test"—which is comprised of riding the horse first at a walk, then a trot, then a canter, and then maybe even a gallop, back and forth across the ditch, weaving among trees on one side and circling on the polo field on the other. Ideally, I am on a looped rein, one-handed, and the horse has to find his own balance and move his own feet. I simply love the feeling I get when a horse can pass this test of self-carriage. In fact, many of my other favorite things for a horse to do—such as exercising in sets and being ridden bitless—also foster independent movement.

Training Tip: Often, all we need to do is to tell the horse where to go and how fast to get there. **//**

C

D

spiral, square, rectangle, serpentine, figure eight, the letter "D," or the whole alphabet (the list is endless!)—and let your horse adjust his own footwork. Thinking about it this way fosters self-carriage and encourages the rider to "do less." It is fair to say that from the horse's perspective usually doing less, especially with your hands, is always a good thing.

Understanding Equine Motivation

Horses, in their interactions with humans, are primarily motivated by *safety, comfort, play,* and *food.* If a horse doesn't feel safe, his brain is unable to learn effectively (same would be true for humans, dogs, and all other mammals who have ever been studied). Providing for basic needs and not over-facing your horse are, therefore, the first steps in training. Anxiety—on either side—is the enemy of partnership.

Horses instinctually desire comfort, which is why a fundamental training principle is "make what is correct easy and what is incorrect hard." Finding the right timing of pressure (which the horse moves away from) and release (which is the horse's reward) is a lifelong skill to work on. And there (I even used it!) is the dreaded word: *work*! We need to remember that in the end, everything we do with horses is play. Not many of us use horses for true work anymore, at least in the developed world. And horses love to play! Bringing their innate curiosity to the fore, and developing a sense of fun in all we do with them, brings more rewards than

★ The Training Triangle

Picture your life with a horse as a triangle. On top, appropriately, is the horse. A successful relationship requires a suitable horse for whatever it is you wish to do together: breed, conformation, previous training, and personality all come into play. The bottom left of the triangle is the rider. Is the rider willing to put in the work and willing to learn? The bottom right of the triangle is time. The time facet includes patience, performing quality repetition, and having the honesty to not overestimate your or your horse's capabilities at any given point in time (and not let ego get in the way). //

★ How Much to Expect

As horses proceed in their training, a new dilemma arises—and that is how much to expect. We take so much for granted every time we are around a trained horse, both on the ground and mounted. We take it for granted that the horse is going to respond predictably to the pressure we apply—for example, to go forward—whether it be on his head via a lead rope or on his side via our leg. I try to keep in mind that there may be some things for any particular horse on any particular day I still need to ask permission for. I try to remember to be respectful. //

/ **3.3** / My opinion, for what it's worth, on riding polo ponies, and all horses, is that you have to pay strict attention to the order of the aids: first legs, then seat, then hands. As humans we have to practice not being hands-first. Riding bitless, like in this bitless rope side-pull (which looks like a halter), is a great way to reinforce not always resorting to hands-first thought patterns and muscle memory.

grinding on their weaknesses to make them better at a "job."

One of my favorite ways to play with a horse is to teach him to follow my feet. It begins with simple leading, where your feet moving forward and stopping are learned by the horse to be the primary cues. Then I add backing up, and changes of speed and direction. Since most horses are taught to lead exclusively off pressure on their head, the halter initially needs to act as a reinforcement, but I find most horses adapt fairly quickly. And I think they like it.

You can also transition to using your feet for cues to walk, trot, and canter in the round pen (having spent a considerable amount of time pretending I was a horse in my youth, this comes naturally to me!). Playing this way feels grounded, like the energy between the human and horse just settles and relaxes. In my experience, it also seems to translate quite well to communication under saddle.

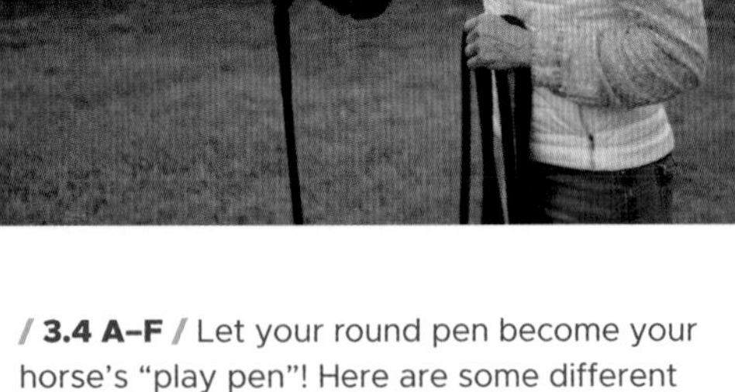

/ 3.4 A–F / Let your round pen become your horse's "play pen"! Here are some different ways to encourage play:

Let your horse adjust to seeing you at the height you'd be on his back, more or less **(A)**. Foster calm moments of no pressure **(B)**. You gotta love a listening ear **(C)**. Build self-carriage in a nice round canter **(D)**. I can't wait to ride that trot **(E)**. You might find someone following you when your "play session" is done **(F)**.

E

F

Despite food being, for most horses, the least motivating factor of the four I named on page 36, it is one of the most commonly used. I personally do not like using food treats for training purposes as I feel it puts horses in the wrong frame of mind to learn. In my experience it "revs them up" by seemingly activating their sympathetic nervous system—which is linked to their responses in the fight or flight mode, and is not the side of the brain we prefer our horses to use when in our company. Constantly giving a horse enticing snacks is basically relaying to him, "It is okay to think of me as a food source only. Don't really worry about what else I am doing or trying to learn with you."

Treats are also a pleasure shortcut—it takes much more time to satisfy your horse's favorite itchy spot. (Do you know where your horse most likes to be rubbed? Hint: usually it is somewhere around the forehead, ears, or poll, although withers and rump are common spots, too.) Try using the touch of a comforting hand as a reward, and notice how much calmer your horse becomes, for example, than when he is aggressively nosing around you for a treat. We want our horses to always associate being with us with being tranquil; we want them to be comforted by us. Here is a horsemanship challenge: Practice finding your horse's favorite rubbing spot every time you halter or bridle him. It will enrich your relationship—and isn't that what it all is really about? For can you imagine being led around all day

★ Treat-Free Zone

I actually prohibit use of treats during my veterinary work for the same reasons I don't use them in training. I want my patients calm and giving me their full attention so we can both focus on the task at hand. I don't want them thinking about food. I do my best to use my horsemanship skills to persuade my patients to do as I ask, instead of resorting to treats. And in my acupuncture-dominated veterinary practice it is really more a requirement than a preference—because of the neurotransmitter activation necessary to achieve the full benefits and therapeutic effects of acupuncture, the horse's parasympathetic nervous system must predominate during the needling process. //

★ Exceptions to the Rule

As with most issues, there is another viewpoint when it comes to the use of food in training, so here it is: chewing and grinding food is a parasympathetic (calming) activity in most contexts. You know this intuitively when you watch a horse's attitude and posture when grazing. When eating grass or hay, they exude contentment. And you can also sense that horses don't want to eat when they are overexcited. This has a lot to do with the action of the muscles used in masticating fibrous food. But for some horses, even giving them a treat (which they don't really chew) will still make them quieter. You should certainly experiment with your horse to see if in some situations he will take a treat, take a breath, and still his feet. Goal accomplished. //

by the head? It truly is amazing the horse submits. To make it a little more palatable to him, take an extra 10 seconds to caress his poll or ears or forehead.

Another way to think about spoiling a horse with food is that relying on treats for good behavior is like being a grandparent, instead of a parent: Grandparents can spoil their grandchildren, and then give them back after the fun is had; they do not have to live with the consequences of any of their actions. Parenting is about building a more integral and productive relationship, based on good decision-making among hard choices. Which role do you want to play for your horse?

I must add that at *the end* of any kind of training session, I am completely on board with using treats as a reward, but timing is everything. When your time with your horse for the day is drawing to a close, the halter is almost off, and he is about to be left alone to ponder his good fortune, *that's* the time for a treat.

I recently noted a circular evolution of language in how we speak of starting horses: In Shakespeare's *The Tempest* there is a reference to "the cocked ear of an unbacked colt." Then centuries of "breaking" horses was championed by the American cowboys (north) and gauchos (south). Currently, natural horsemanship methods have restored the term "backing" into style. Words do matter—our language mirrors humans' relationships with horses. Hopefully we keep evolving, linearly now rather than circling back, to be more and more humane in our talk and actions.

// Winning Point

If I start feeling impatience or anger rise in me (which does happen—I am only human) I hit the "pause button" on whatever I am doing with a horse. If I am riding, I halt and talk out loud to myself (usually starting off by apologizing

/ 3.5 / Give yourself a day a week, or at least a day a month, to replenish your relationship with your horse—like couples therapy—and do something together you both truly enjoy. Adam and I are on two homebreds for an experience we all four enjoy.

to my horse, which somehow always seems to get their attention) and then problem-solve the situation. If I am on the ground, I take a deep breath, and if that is not enough to set those negative emotions aside, I turn away from my horse and let the feelings out with an exasperated sigh or stomp of my foot. Since "training" is what we do in our *every* interaction with our horses, it is imperative we try our best to get it right. To bring the best out of our horses we have to bring the best out of ourselves. So here is the training mindset to remember: flexible; in the moment. The Zen master would ask, "Just who is training who here?" //

★ The Well-Bred and Well-Fed Phenomenon

This is a common problem because we all want our horses to look nice and behave well. Sometimes those two objectives are at odds with each other. My advice on how to avoid the sedative drug trap (which I unfortunately witness all too often in clients trying to make their horses safer to ride) and instead keep it natural:

1. Feed a high-quality hay and minimize or completely avoid processed grain.
2. Develop your horsemanship skills: Watch their ears and move their feet.
3. Supplement wisely (see p. 169 for more on this).
4. Try a Liquid Titanium® therapeutic mask for a calming effect.
5. Learn some simple acupressure, massage, and stretching exercises to decrease sympathetic tone (the condition of a muscle when the tone is maintained predominantly by impulses from the sympathetic nervous system).

end *of* chapter 3

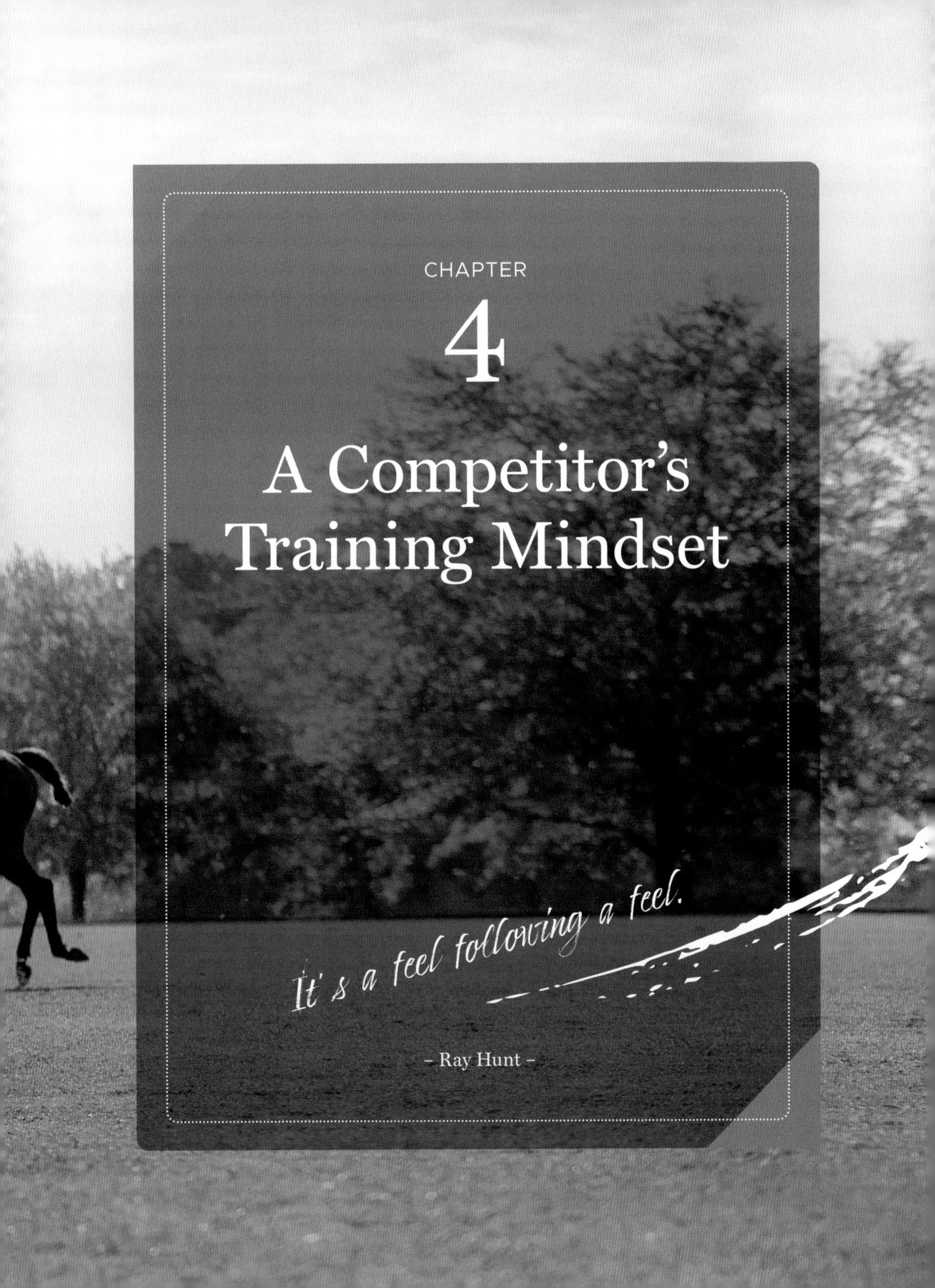

CHAPTER

4

A Competitor's Training Mindset

It's a feel following a feel.

– Ray Hunt –

// A Competitor's Training Mindset

Pretend You Have a Mallet in Your Hand

I believe that trust is the most important ingredient toward a successful partnership between horse and rider on the playing field or in the show ring. This trust is most complete when based on a layered foundation of training and shared experience.

When we were breeding at New Haven Farm, there were times when Shelley would find me in the round pen, looking uncertain aboard a freshly started three-year-old. Her suggestion, "Pretend you have a mallet in your hand and want to make some plays," was the perfect antidote to my uncertainty. Still today, having the comfort of a mallet as well as the orientation of a ball helps direct my riding in a manner that horses seem to understand. Perhaps they feel that I am more relaxed, more confident. Maybe it's as simple as lifting my eyes, *zooming out* from the top of the horse's neck and trying to perceive every foot shift, and viewing the general objective of our partnership. In this way the training process becomes aspirational

CHAPTER

and my competitive experience hopefully enhances the baby steps *we* take together.

"The process doesn't have to look like the product," Pat Parelli once told me. And I keep this sharply in mind as I look for variation, and *games to play,* all along the way. Today, I am much more likely to "change it up" with an individual horse and not feel compelled to follow my old training, riding, and horse management routines.

But where did these routines come from? Essentially from observation and then "doing it": making mistakes and then learning from them. If our powers of observation are one of our best learning tools, then I learned a lot through the years...and from a variety of different sources. I kept my eyes and ears open. And I asked lots of questions of the owners and managers of the breeding and training operations with which I had involvement. These included *El Pucara* in Trenque Lauquen, Argentina, where I worked for Hector Barrantes out of college; King Bros in Sheridan, Wyoming, where Mike Morton raised, trained, and sold K-3 brand polo ponies; Wildwood Farms in Memphis, Tennessee, owned by Lee and Melanie (Smith) Taylor, who sometimes sold, and more often loaned me, excellent ponies from their breeding; and Isinya HDC here in Aiken, South Carolina, where my friend and former teammate Owen Rinehart (also a 10-goal player) runs a successful breeding and training operation. All of these people I consider mentors in their own way. Additionally, I studied the "teams" (of horses, players, and staff) that I competed with all over the world. I analyzed how

★ The Evolution of Knowledge

Early in my career, I was heavily influenced by Argentine grooms who had worked at the upper levels of the sport, say for players competing in the Argentine Open. *If they did it this way, then who was I to say or do differently?* This pertained to trot sets, when to ride singles or "give the horses air," if and whether to muzzle horses in their stalls, and sometimes feeding less or no hay prior to matches. Many of these *petiseros* were excellent horsemen, but they had learned from a fairly rough horse culture and heritage. With time and learning, gradually I (and the *petiseros* too) gained the confidence to make adaptations away from this traditional (Argentine) style of doing things. And, interestingly, the best Argentine barns today take a far more humane approach to the care and treatment of their horses. //

top grooms and players interacted with their horses on and off the field.

I also exchanged ideas with the trainers who I bought horses from (I always made sure to send them a photo if their horse went on to win a BPP prize under me). I got to witness first-hand Shelley's performance and intuitively-based veterinary approach. And, of course, I had my own hands-on work experience grooming as a kid in order to get to play.

So, there were many sources for my own, constantly evolving, "horsemanship routine." Along my path, indeed anyone's path, it is about taking what works for us and our horses, integrating those aspects into *our* routines, and leaving behind what does not fit. It is also about being

★ Learning to Feel the Horse

As a kid working out of my grandparents' barn, I recall our veterinarian's infrequent visits for his shock of white hair and an aroma of Absorbine Veterinary Liniment. When Dr. Thibeault came to evaluate a lameness on one of my dad's horses, he seemed always to prescribe a gel-cast (which he would administer) and some time off. PDQ, a Thoroughbred gelding that was my favorite pony, was no exception. Dr. Thibeault prescribed two weeks' rest, and then a gradual leg-up program with lots of walking and trotting before playing him again.

I was intent on getting PDQ back as soon as possible to play in an upcoming tournament. So, after the recommended rest period, I began working him each day at a walk and trot—like Dr. Thibeault had suggested.

One day I rode across the Ipswich River to where there was nice track surrounding Bird's Field on the other side. PDQ still had his white gel-cast on. As I began posting, I kept an eye on the 6-goal player, Steve (Stevie) Orthwein, who was stick-and-balling his own ponies on the field. There was always something to learn from a good, experienced player!

PDQ and I must have trotted two or three laps around the track, before Stevie called over: "Hey, Adam, that horse isn't getting any sounder!"

Mortified, I slowed to a walk, and PDQ and I returned across the river to the barn. He had the rest of the season off. And I promised myself to feel the horse next time, and not let myself be blinded by the supposed urgency of my preferred rehab goals. //

adaptable. Striving to maintain a *beginner's mind*—an attitude of openness and eagerness—makes us better listeners and allows us to keep learning, always.

More recently, my observations are related to the general field of natural horsemanship. I realize this classification could be fraught, but suffice it to say that there is very little I don't like from the exposure I've had with some of its practitioners, such as Buck Brannaman, Pat Parelli, Monty Roberts, Julie Robbins, and Tink Elordi. Many of their suggestions and practices, I have adapted toward my own routine. This stuff was new to me when I was first exposed to it in the early 1990s, but the common-sense concept of working *with* the horse's natural instincts jived with my own. Plus, I was always looking for a competitive edge.

As my tableau of observations grew—and I continued to make my own mistakes—increasingly, I came to trust my own intuition. "If I think it, *try it*," has become a motto I aim to live by when it comes to an individual horse's preparation. This could mean a change of bit because the idea keeps crossing my mind (sometimes there's a picture in my mind of the horse in a different bit), a day or two off, or a pre-match trot in a bitless hackamore with some leg-yielding patterns in a corral rather than "blowing one out" on the polo field. When I have the confidence to try these ideas, usually I'm happy I did.

★ Focus on Good Riding

I heard an instructor say once that "stadium jumping is like dressage with a few jumps thrown in the way." And I have always thought of polo as good riding with a few hits of the ball to execute along the way. In both situations—indeed in most equestrian sports—the focus on "good riding," which to me essentially means being balanced and in sync with your horse, helps make whatever challenges your sport presents easier to negotiate. //

Doing It the Way We Learned

Last summer in Wyoming, I sat with one of my mentors on his porch overlooking

★ Wyoming-Bred

One K-3 bred mare became one of our favorites. Rio arrived on the farm from Wyoming as a two-year-old, and it was Shelley who rode her first and continued her training. In 2001 Rio was featured in the PBS Nature Series Horse in Sport. They attached a head-cam to my polo helmet and filmed her first high-goal match in Florida at age six; they also filmed the care she received (including acupuncture) back in the barn before and after her debut. She went on to play the 2004 Argentine Open, and then win the 2006 US Open. She is the oldest horse I have played in tournament polo, at age 24. Unfortunately, she could not hold a pregnancy. Currently, she is the oldest retired horse on our farm. //

the Big Horn Mountains. Mike Morton, retired and closing in on his eightieth birthday, asked me: "Did you like the way I trained all those K-3 horses you bought from me?"

Mike had tallied a list of 28 horses that Shelley and I had purchased from him at the King Bros Ranch, since we began going there in the early nineties. Urchin and Rio had played in the Argentine Open in 2004. Several had won BPP prizes, and many had been sold on to successful careers with other polo players.

"Of course," I responded, "otherwise I wouldn't have bought them."

Mike explained that he'd asked because he'd started those horses the "old-fashioned way"—the way he had learned while working as a wrangler in the 1960s. "I know you like the natural horsemanship stuff," he said, "and I tried it, but I had more success doing it the way I first learned."

Mike recalled participating in a Ray Hunt colt-starting clinic: "There was a lot of prejudice in this country when the horse whisperers come out, but I thought, 'What a great thing they're doing by introducing people to snaffles and power steering.' But Ray savvy'd stuff the old-time cowboys did and then took it to a much higher level. One of the best men I've ever seen with a rope. But he had something you can't teach...Ray had a sixth sense...maybe even a seventh. He could change a horse's mind! He could anticipate *everything*. The problem for the students at that clinic was that they could never *be* Ray Hunt."

I knew what Mike was talking about. I had felt the same way when I watched

Buck Brannaman or Pat Parelli working with a horse at the end of a rope. Their timing was perfect, instinctive. They didn't need to think about it. I learned quickly that I could never *be* them. I could improve, and I would, but even spending 1,000 hours on groundwork would never get me to their level. And that's why Shelley's suggestion to "Pretend you have a mallet in your hand" was so instructive—because I believe we're better trainers for keeping our strengths foremost in mind.

Mike, for example, felt most comfortable doing things the way he had learned from some top hands up in the Bighorn Mountains. He reeled off some men's names: Bob Laferty, Chuck Best, Jerry Landon, Ike Fordyce, Archie McCarty, and Joe Back. "Everybody has ways of breakin' horses, but *cowboyin'* is knowin' when to push a horse and when to back off; knowin' when to crowd cattle and when not to." Mike named the best trainer he knew as "the advantage of Western influence—big country and lots of cattle. I'm teaching my horses all day long with cattle; after that, polo is no big deal."

Training Never Ends

On our polo farm in Aiken, between the ages of five and seven we add an important layer to a horse's early foundation—exposing horses to the demands of competition. (Since most of the horses we bought in Wyoming, from Mike and others, were age five or younger, they also received this stage of the training process.) This involves

/ 4.1 / The training starts back at the barn with saddling and bridling. This mare, Kombucha, makes everything easy.

★ Stop and Start Over

As Shelley referenced in chapter 3 (p. 23), sometimes we humans can let our emotions get in the way. This happens when we are rushed for time, are frustrated that our horse doesn't "get it," or when we carry unrealistic expectations for our partnership. Unfortunately, this is when pressure can, often unwittingly, turn into punishment. The POP of a whip in a moment of anger—for something that already happened—is rarely effective, because the horse doeesn't understand what he's being punished for. In Ray Hunt's words, "Don't try to go through something bad and come out good....stop and start over." //

introducing a young pony to the feeling of immersing in the flow of the game, reacting play-by-play. This part comes naturally for me, so I can let my body lead. Since I fully trust my own *feel* on the horse (especially with a mallet in my hand), I try to stop thinking about ways to improve everything and let the game be the teacher. My horses can ask questions: *Do you really want me to try to squeeze through that traffic? Don't you think this is fast enough? Didja' see that freaky looking mower over there?* Sometimes the horse is actually teaching ME, and often, these are lessons in humility.

The homebreds that I play today have all, in their own way, contributed to the lore of the New Haven Farm training program. And it is always the hiccups, rather than smooth sailings, which lend themselves to the most frequent retelling.

One cool morning during winter green horse chukkers at Owen Rinehart's facility Isinya HDC, Tequila's daughter, Rum Runner, demonstrated her cat-like quickness by disappearing out from under me while banking to the right. One moment I was out over her neck reaching for the ball on the offside (vaguely aware of some traffic ahead on the right) and the next...the cold, hard ground was approaching fast. Some of my peers in that practice still refer to Rum Runner as "PBR" for the case of Pabst Blue Ribbon I purchased and distributed later as penance for leaving the tack. (In polo's "green horse circles," there is a tradition that if you fall off without your horse going down, you owe everyone a case of beer. I'm not sure where this tradition started, but when it's my turn, I make sure to pay up quickly so as not to tempt fate and risk another tumble.) The crazy thing was that in the previous chukker, when another rider had fallen, I had been the first to start joshing about what kind of beer

★ Umwelt

When we're talking about the perspective of our horses, I found a new favorite word in Elizabeth Kolbert's captivating piece, "The Strange and Secret Ways That Animals Perceive the World," published in *The New Yorker* in June of 2022. She writes:

> *Every animal is enclosed within its own sensory bubble, perceiving but a tiny sliver of an immense world. There is a wonderful word for this sensory bubble—Umwelt. It was defined and popularized by the Baltic German zoologist Jakob von Uexkull in 1909. Umwelt comes from the German word for 'environment.' But Uexkull didn't use it to refer to an animal's surroundings. Instead an Umwelt is specifically the part of those surroundings that an animal can sense and experience—its perceptual world. A tick, questing for mammalian blood, cares about body heat, the touch of hair, and the odor of butyric acid that emanates from skin. It doesn't care about other stimuli, and probably doesn't know that they exist. Every Umwelt is limited; it just doesn't feel that way. Each one feels all-encompassing to those who experience it. Our Umwelt is all we know, and so we easily mistake it for all there is to know. This is an illusion that every creature shares. Humans, however, possess the unique capacity to appreciate the Umwelten of other species.*

And so, when we really try to see things from our horse's viewpoint, we are considering their *umwelt*. It is almost like looking at things from a friend's perspective, but now our friend is a different species. This is something Shelley acknowledges every time she sits on a young horse (see Chapter 3) or steps in, or out, of an equestrian patient's space while administering acupuncture (see Chapter 7). And it's something I need to work on.

How can I work on this? I guess by paying attention to the small things each time I'm with these animals. Being observant may be the best way to listen to our animals. How does he step through a gate or into his stall? How does he interact with his pasturemates? Can I keep myself from rushing when I'm around him? Or, if I feel myself in a rush, can I learn to step away and come back another time when I can be fully present? Most of my mistakes, at least on a horse's back, seem to happen when I am rushing to get through something. It just doesn't work for horses. Like us, they possess their own distinct personalities, so it's not right for us to think we can ride and maintain them all as if they were coming out of the same cookie cutter.

Today, I think I have a better sense of my horses' unique perspectives (their *umwelten*) than at any point since I began riding. Sometimes I can just see my horses thinking out loud: "That branch wasn't there yesterday!" "C'mon, gimme a little scoop of barley." "That fly is ANNOYING!" "It's not like I started it!" "He won't care if I stop to poop." And sometimes I think I can hear their thoughts. I guess it comes down to listening to them as best we can.

The process of imagining what could be running through our horses' heads, of appreciating and trying to understand their perspective, is valuable. Our horse's sensory bubble is a fascinating thing to contemplate. Perhaps it is only through understanding the limits of our own *umwelt*, that we can further appreciate theirs.

he should buy the group. I don't know what I was thinking—it wasn't like me to be heckling like that—but Rum Runner taught me my lesson.

The thing about training, whatever your discipline, is that the process never really ends. Except for match time (which you will read about later), every time I sit on a horse—he could be 3 or 23—I'm trying to improve things just a little bit more. Thus, this training continues for both horse and rider, with communications being sent back and forth, until the day one of us retires from our respective careers. The late 9-goal Hall of Famer Harold Barry said, "It takes 40 years to become a horseman—20 to realize you don't know anything, and 20 to start learning." While I'm not sure where I am on this curve, I *have* learned that it's with mallet in hand that I feel most adept at building successful partnerships with my equine teammates.

Letting Go

I have often felt the paradox of caring deeply for the horses I compete, and yet needing to forget about them, in some sense, in order to play my best. I believe there exists a *training* mindset and a *competitive* one, and that it is important to distinguish between the two. "Forgetting about" my horse *does not* mean ignoring his *feel*, or pretending I'm riding a motorcycle, or treating all horses alike. It means trusting a connection with your horse to the point of *letting go*. In other words, appreciating that I have done everything in my power

/ 4.2 / The relaxed atmosphere of the farm provides an ideal locale for training young polo ponies.

to prepare that horse for the sport, physically and mentally, and freeing myself of unnecessary concerns in order to *play*. The development of this partnership can take years, countless rides in different settings and circumstances, hundreds of practice sessions. Or it can take no time at all. In some instances where I have to rely on borrowed horses to play an important match, such as international friendlies or substituting (as I did in the finals of the 2011 Joe Barry Memorial), trust is the only option.

For me, it is more challenging to leave the training mindset behind when playing a horse that we have bred and raised. Since Shelley and I have, quite literally, been training the horse since day one, the hopes and expectations that develop naturally with each homebred can complicate things. Nevertheless, the best horses I am playing today are the sons and daughters of mares I competed on at the height of my career. Not only is it a great group, but there is nothing more rewarding than getting to participate in both the training and competitive cycles of one

/ 4.3 / (Left to right): Dionysus, Pele, and Nureyev ("Nuri")—three homebred colts.

animal. For most competitive riders, it is possible to shift between these two states. But for many, myself included, it is difficult to leave behind the training mindset before important competitions.

Our sons' favorite soccer camp in Santa Barbara, California—ONE.soccer-schools—has the slogan *Always Training.* I like the logic, at least when it comes to our boys juggling a soccer ball and working on their left foot; but, in relation to a career competing to win on horses, in my opinion, *always training* can be more of a liability than an asset. The "training" is the practice part of things, done back at the barn or on the schooling field. It is conscious and calculated, with decisions being made for improvement's sake. It is a hard thing to shut off, but just as athletes should free their minds from technical, "how to" thoughts while in the moment of competition so, too, should a rider free her mind from the training mentality utilized in the schooling ring. In other words, it is time to play/compete/perform with your eyes, your breath, and the feel of the horse under you. Quieting your analytical, training mind can enhance performance for you and your horse.

On Breeding

I joke that breeding horses taught me to like geldings. While Shelley and I had, over the years, raised the odd foal on our farm, it was really 2010 when we decided to give breeding a try at any scale. We owned several excellent retired mares, and I was considering slowing down tournament play, which could mean more time for me on the farm to help with the young ones. So the idea of getting a foal or two out of some of my favorites was appealing.

Up to that point, if I was trying prospects to buy, I wouldn't even look at a gelding. With a few notable exceptions—Wyatt Earp, and later, Ming and

★ Wait to Compete

We should be breeding and training horses for long, healthy careers in their sports. Many of our horses enjoyed competitive careers of over 10 years. I take my time when it comes to choosing the moment to start playing a horse in tournament polo. There is no problem in waiting an extra few months, or even a year, if it is going to mean a more settled horse and a long, healthy, athletic career. //

Vee—I only played mares. I loved their sensitivity and athleticism, and I was aware of the potential for breeding when their playing days were over. I was a "mare guy"...or so I thought.

That spring we bred five mares—Pumbaa, Bag Lady, Josephine, Haley, and Chlöe—to two different stallions. And, roughly 11 months later, five male foals touched down on New Haven Farm. In addition to my cumulative disappointment regarding gender—the number of male horses on the farm had, more or less overnight, increased fivefold—our "mom-and-pop operation" was also somewhat overwhelmed by the new numbers and the individual attention these foals required.

So, that season we chose not to breed back any of the mares, and never again bred more than three in any given year. It was a quick transition to what Jeff Hall, another professional player, called "boutique breeding"—going for quality, not quantity, with just a few.

But even boutique had its challenges, namely that I became so attached to these homebreds (their mothers represented the cream of my playing career) that I didn't want to sell them. And given I was well into my fifties, breeding with the purpose of me playing their offspring seemed to defy logic—I'm rarely fully confident on horses until they're eight or nine years old. (And, by 11 or 12, they're even better!) Given my age as well as the fact that our children weren't playing, the math didn't add up. So we bred small numbers for four more years, and then we called it quits.

And I kept playing.

Today, I feel like the beneficiary of those breeding years. Five of my favorite horses are from our breeding, and I could never have afforded to purchase ponies of their quality in the latter stages of my career. Most of these homebreds were started under saddle by Shelley, as well as Aiken-based trainers Julie Nicholson and Don Healey. And one—LolliBopp—was, very cautiously, backed by me. Being involved with the entire process of a horse's career—from his big-kneed suckling days, to weaning, to starting in the round-pen, to training, to playing keep-away, to joining practices, and to eventually one day competing in tournament polo—is a unique and rewarding experience.

It's been almost seven years since the last foal, LolliBopp, was born on our farm. Presently, and for mostly emotional reasons, we are contemplating breeding two mares this coming spring. Perhaps an owner's decision *if*, *when*, and *whether* to breed does have more to do with emotion than logic. *If* we breed Sky this March to my favorite polo stallion, River Dance (who stands conveniently across the street at Isinya), *and* she delivers a healthy baby, the foal would be the first, third-generation polo pony we will have bred...and probably ever will. Like mother (Tequila), like daughter (Sky), like granddaughter? Writing this, my mind already skips excitedly to potential names.

Of the original five stud-colts that foaled back in 2011, one passed due to birthing complications, one foal-and-mother pair were given to a great home in Texas with the dam's former owner, and three of them went on to play happily in competitive polo, with me in the saddle. One of these original homebreds is among the best horses I've *ever* played, of either sex, at any point in my career. I may not be able to show him the way I once did, but I can still *feel it*—and he's got it.

So, when it comes to liking geldings, breeding made a believer out of me.

”

The proper bit is the one that the horse goes best in.

On Bitting

Bitting, like many things in the horse world, is a subjective matter, and, at least for most equestrian sports, the goal is comfort and responsiveness in the dance between horse and rider.

I realize that bitting can be a sensitive topic and that some caring horse people may raise their eyebrows at using a Barry gag or draw reins. Indeed, there are many expert riders who prefer only to use snaffles. And I respect this choice. But I would rather see an easy-to-stop, collected horse in a more severe bit than someone sawing away before a jump or on the polo field in a lighter bit that the horse does not respect. *A more severe bit is not necessarily harsher if, in the hands of the rider, the horse is softer.* This equation varies according to horse, rider, and competitive goals.

My initial experience riding all day, with the horse's development foremost in mind, was the apprenticeship I mentioned earlier in these pages for Hector Barrantes at his breeding and training farm *El Pucara.* My first morning on the farm I was given a saddle, two bridles (one gag and one pelham), and pointed toward eight horses milling in the run-in dirt corrals.

"Ride them every day, and always have a reason for what you are doing," were Hector's instructions.

Today, I have more bridles than horses. In addition to 30-odd complete polo bridles hanging on our double-sided divider wall in the tack room, there are three small duffel bags and a wooden ammo box all bulging with bits in our barn. The red duffel, my travel bag for away tournaments, carries my favorite gags that are not already hung on bridles. The blue one has curb bits and extras like Weymouths (both ported and Mullen mouthpieces), pelhams, and broken pelhams of various kinds. And the green duffel contains exercise bits—snaffles, Kimberwicks, wonder bits, an Argentine *cocohero,* a Chilean snaffle, and the odd small-ring gag like my Hitchcock or the tiny half-moon that I grew up playing PDQ in. Shelley calls me a "gear queer," and I am guilty as charged. There is more than a little collector's pride in the array of sweet iron, copper, and nickel mouthpieces from different eras and regions of the globe. I would like to think that 35 years' worth of experience has taught me a more nuanced approach to bitting and the best connection between my hands and the horse's brain and feet. But Hector's instructions from 1987 still ring true: "Always have a reason for what you are doing."

The competitor in me wants my horse to react quickest. If my goal as an athlete is to *look and react,* then my goal as a rider is to communicate efficiently in order to give my horse every chance possible of arriving first—to slow down and turn, to jump out in order to win the position on an opponent. For me, when I am in the fray, most of this communication is instinctive. To this day, I have more trouble instructing polo equitation than almost any other aspect of the game. *I don't know what I do, I just do it.* The more efficiently rider and horse communicate—through seat, legs, and reins—the more time and space is created for executing a play on the ball. Argentine great Daniel Gonzalez claims that "a polo player's handicap is proportional to the amount of time they give themselves at the ball." And how better to give ourselves time than to have tack and equipment that is correct,

/ 4.4 / In the tackroom are my playing bridles—the bridle wall has two sides, and both sides are almost full **(A)**. Here you see an assortment of gags on the left-hand side, and mostly curb bits (like pelhams) on the right. The exercise bridles are in my barn aisle **(B)**. They are what I use to exercise and take sets with the horses on a daily basis. "Sunny's bridle" is on the far right.

comfortable, and contributing to an accurate level of responsiveness?

American 10-goaler and legendary horseman Tommy Wayman coached me to "play the horse in the bit he plays best in." For illustration, he added some cowboy hyperbole: "If I have to hang a kitchen sink on my horse's head in order for him to play his best, well then I'll ..." He never did this (that I know of), but I took his point.

I've always liked the rationale of having the horse light in my hand, even if it

meant having him in more bridle. But I've known many horses for whom less was more. I remember a mare named Halo that came into polo from the racetrack. I was loaning her to a teammate one season in Aiken, and after a practice or two, he came to me convinced that "she needs the lightest bit you have." I was a little skeptical since I'd been playing her for several years, but I let him choose a full-cheeked snaffle from my green bit bag. And the mare made an immediate, marked improvement on the field. Maybe it gave her the confidence that she could lean on something a little, or she preferred direct pressure rather than the pulley of a gag or leverage of a pelham. The next Florida season, still in that snaffle, Halo went from being an occasional spare in my string to becoming one of my very best. At the time, she was already 12 years old; she'd had plenty of training and polo. She was the same mare, but it took the snaffle. A lesson I won't forget.

The exercise bridles, which I use on a daily basis on all my horses, live on a row of hooks in our barn aisle. These are mostly snaffles (three-piece, loose ring, and egg-butt) rigged with split reins or mecate reins and slobber straps; a Western, rope side-pull; a nylon bitless hackamore; and a three-piece, sweet-metal, Western grazing bit (that I call "Sunny's bridle") with small copper rings in the middle for the horse's tongue to play with. Sunny Hale gave me the grazing bit as a thank you gift for loaning her two horses, Spy and Rio, for the US Open we played together in 2003.

★ Ode to Sunny

On February 26, 2017, the horse world lost one of its greatest. Sunset "Sunny" Hale was a horse lover, a competitor, a teammate, an inspiration, and a friend. "Let's do this," she used to say, and indeed, her pioneering accomplishments were remarkable.

In 2000, she made history by becoming the first woman polo player to win the US Open. She achieved the highest handicap (5 goals) of any American female player to date. She is the author of five books about horses, game preparation, and being a champion in the sport of polo (regardless of the results).

Sunny was instrumental to the rise of modern women's polo, creating the US Women's Open, which is now played annually at the National Polo Center in Wellington, Florida, as well as the parallel women's handicap system. She created the *American Polo Horse Association*, a registry of American-born polo ponies intended to catalog on-field successes as well as genetics (and thereby add value to future generations of their offspring). In 2012 Sunny was inducted into the National Cowgirl Hall of Fame alongside fellow trailblazers like Sandra Day O'Connor, Annie Oakley, and Georgie O'Keeffe. Sunny was born in Carmel, California, so the Cowgirl Hall of Fame's motto—*Women who shape the West change the world*—fits her like a glove.

Shortly after her passing, Sunny was also inducted into the United States Polo Hall of Fame. //

Tragically, Sunny passed away prematurely, in 2017. "Sunny's bridle" continues to remind me of her passion for horses and the sport of polo. And it is my go-to for a horse's initial introduction to the feel of a curb chain.

For both practice games and tournament matches, I play my horses in their "polo bridles." These are also the times I experiment with slight tweaks to their polo bridles—a different curb chain, a different noseband. The bits are mostly the same two I was given back at *El Pucara*—gags and pelhams—with the addition of broken pelhams and full-bridles (usually a ported Weymouth with a twisted sweet-iron bridoon). Occasionally, there is a snaffle in the mix—Halo, Pele, Sasebo, and maybe now Bondi all played or play in them—but this is generally not the rule. When Buck Brannaman worked as a young horse trainer for Sun South, a polo organization in Florida, he was given a group of young horses to practice and he played every one of them in a snaffle and straight reins. "If I can't get them to play well for me in a snaffle, then I'm not a good enough trainer," he told me. And, I heard they all played well. When it comes to game time and the objective is to win, attaining the edge in responsiveness may necessitate a different choice.

There are all different ways I use to arrive at the right bit for the horse...and for me. Some horses clearly don't like certain mouthpieces, and they will demonstrate their displeasure by shaking their heads, gnawing on the bit itself, or schooling with less responsiveness. In addition to having their teeth floated regularly,

★ Simplest Means of Communication

Choosing a bit to ride in on a certain day is a little like choosing a gear for a bicycle: You want to keep the same pressure (from either the hand in the case of the bits or from the legs in the case of the bicycle gear) regardless of the difficulty of the task at hand. The correct bit should make communication simplest for the specific activity at hand. For example, one of our mares rode best in an enclosed space in a bitless side-pull, singled on the polo field in a snaffle, and played in a gag. //

I check their mouths frequently, especially when experimenting with a new bridle that may mean a different point of contact. With gags and snaffles, I like to hang them slightly loose so that the horse has an opportunity to pick up the bit, and so that the release can be quick and clean.

If I had to choose my dream bit today, it would be the gag I use on my favorite gelding, Vee. It's a medium-ring, sweet-iron gag, with a fat smooth mouthpiece, inlaid with copper strips. The core of the mouthpiece has been filled with lead (a Tommy Wayman idea). This gag was crafted by Tom Balding in Sheridan, Wyoming, and sent to me for trial when I was 10 goals. I gave it the big thumbs-up, and have been happily using it ever since. It's sweet and heavy, and Vee carries it like it's part of him.

// Winning Point

Our learning can come from many sources and experiences, and is often specific to our unique situations, but it is all of our jobs to integrate what we hear, see, and feel into a system that functions for us and our horses. Like training, this process never really ends, but ideally it is always improving. Reflecting on a career of riding horses in tournament competitions, I see now—even though I may not have realized it at the time—that in almost every case my personal polo goals went hand-in-hand with the best interests of my horses. //

end *of* chapter 4

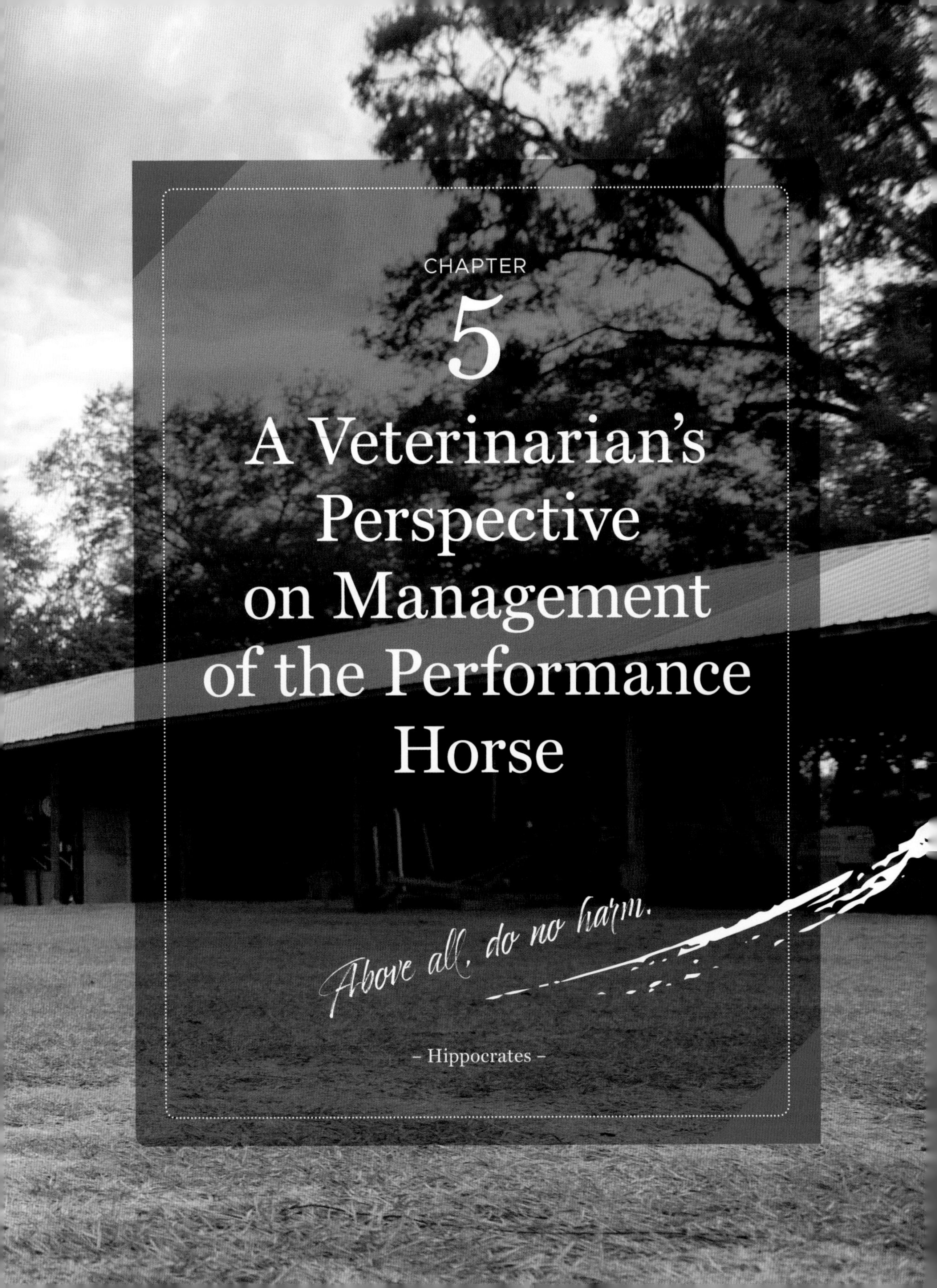

CHAPTER

5

A Veterinarian's Perspective on Management of the Performance Horse

Above all, do no harm.

– Hippocrates –

// A Veterinarian's Perspective on Management of the Performance Horse

In the field of equine medicine, although I have made mistakes in erring on the side of doing less (for example, starting antibiotics a day or two later than optimal), I have not, to this moment, made a mistake of doing too much (for example, foundering a horse with medication). And I hope never to. I don't think "there is a drug for everything" like many do; I view it more as "there are a lot of drugs out there with good effects, and most have side effects." There is almost always a risk versus benefit ratio I am calculating when I ponder using a drug. Western medicine is by its nature innovative and interventionist. The language is centered around *getting rid of disease*. My medical philosophy incorporates an integrative approach that combines Western medicine with alternative therapies, such as acupuncture and physical therapy, which are by their very nature more natural and homeostatic—their language revolves around *restoring the body to heal itself.*

Early in my career, a veterinarian friend remarked to Adam, "You are so lucky! Shelley will be able to inject your horses' [joints] all the time!"

CHAPTER 5

I was flabbergasted but at an uncharacteristic loss for words as my incredulity muted me. To think some might think the only obstacle in the way of such a decision might be cost! Except in rare cases, I mostly view joint injections as a band-aid, and I can count on two hands the number of our horses who've received them over the 24 years (hundreds of horses and thousands of chukkers) I've been in charge.

Some sports medicine veterinarians are performance-oriented to strive to get the horse to the next competition at all costs; at the other end of the spectrum, some holistically-minded veterinarians prescribe nothing but rest. I believe it is possible to strike a happy balance somewhere in the middle and take the best of both. Personally, being very competitive myself, I enjoy helping equine athletes, and their riders, reach their full potential. I have been fortunate to have a meaningful part of my practice be comprised of Adam's horses and my own, where I truly have no pressure to do anything but exactly what I feel is best for the horse in any given situation. That freedom has taught me a lot about how to make the difficult calls regarding how much to push. And it has helped me understand what makes a winning equine athlete.

I must admit that I harbor one deep prejudice in my veterinary practice: I am against steroid use. Etched in my memory is a canine patient during veterinary school who collapsed and died upon arrival to his appointment. He had been withdrawing from steroid therapy—prescribed for itchy skin—but his own natural system of steroid production was so severely suppressed that he was unable to handle even the mild stress of arriving to the veterinarian's office. It was a tragic lesson I've never forgotten. Even when drug use was unregulated in polo, and all our competitors were on it, I used Winstrol® only once, and I remember it—an older mare I felt would benefit from a dose midseason to stimulate her appetite. Instead of resorting to anabolic steroids regularly, we fed our horses well and conditioned them well and our horses consistently won prizes. And they lasted for years and years at the top of the sport. It comes back to the definition of success in equestrian sport—if longevity is included in this equation, then minimizing interventionist practices and refusing to "medicalize" problems that don't need the "big guns" is vital. It is entirely possible to attain both peak performance and longevity for the equine athlete, and to make it to competitions without sacrificing long-term wellness goals. I know because we've done it. It just takes a different kind of work.

Prevention

It's an old adage but no less true now: *an ounce of prevention is worth a pound of cure*. My ounce of prevention sometimes morphs into pounds or even tons, I freely admit! But it still beats dealing with crises. Much of the "secret sauce" of horse health lies in husbandry practices, such as nutrition, conditioning, and farriery (we explore these in more detail in Chapter 11). From a strict veterinary perspective, however, the best prevention protocol I've found for high-performance athletes is the simple practice of weekly veterinary checks. Catch things early, treat appropriately, and small problems disappear and bigger problems are averted. "Treating appropriately" for me generally consists of using acupuncture and manual therapy, but it can also incorporate physical therapy or medications (or changes to conditioning, nutrition, or farriery). Controlling inflammation through nutrition, herbs, homeopathy, ice, and sometimes drugs is also an integral part of prevention. Long-term thinking is key—unquestionably, some short-term goals (for example, this weekend's competition) will be missed if you want to keep your horse going over the years.

I like to think that "15 is the new 10" when it comes to the ageing of the equine athlete. Just like seven-time-Super-Bowl-winning quarterback Tom Brady defied all expectations of *his* age by following his own nutritional, medical, and conditioning programs, I believe we are on a similar point of breakthrough with horses, where if we play our cards right we'll see more and more horses competing at high levels well into their teens.

We intuitively know there is a difference between *chronological* age and *physiological* age, as ageing is a visible phenomenon (it is measurable medically as well). So how to "slow down the clock" so to speak?

There are four main areas to focus on:

/ **1** / The first is *inflammation*. If you follow any human health research you will be familiar with this one. It applies to horses as well, and the biggest source of inflammation is diet. Paying careful attention to the microbiome includes judicious use of antibiotics and feeding prebiotics to assist the GALT (gut associated lymphatic tissue). Supplementing omega-3 fatty acids also provides a well-documented anti-inflammatory effect. "Natural" feed (more on this later—see p. 165) is key.

/ **2** / A second factor is *stress*, and the good news is that this is very much within our control as caretakers. The most common stressor for horses? Unpredictability in the environment. Make routine your friend.

/ **3** / Thirdly, strive for *symmetry in everything you do*—from the way the horse is ridden to the side he is tacked and mounted. Observe the shape of the horse's hooves, and the development of his muscles, and the evenness of his posture, and address any asymmetries with an appropriate professional.

/ **4** / The last factor is *rest*. Allow the horse sufficient time on a daily, weekly, and a yearly schedule to recuperate physically and mentally.

Addressing these four factors is my prescription to slow down the clock.

Diagnostic Tool Box

Optimizing health can be a frustrating puzzle to figure out. In veterinary medicine it is often the diagnosis that is the hardest part; how I wish sometimes horses could talk! But that's why having a large diagnostic tool box is essential. There are three key elements:

/ **1** / The first is having honest and open communication between the veterinarian and the rider, trainer, groom, or owner—they are a vital source of initial information and accurate feedback. Building a working partnership with shared intentions and mutual support, and trusting each other's decisions, is essential to the health of an animal who doesn't speak human language.

/ **2** / Secondly, performing a thorough physical exam, including neuromuscular assessment, joint range of motion tests, and hoof assessment, is vital. In a world of hi-tech gadgets, the art of palpation and observation has been minimized (certainly on the human side of medicine, and the veterinary side is following suit). But no computer program yet created can take in sensory stimuli like the human brain. A favorite professor of mine once lectured: "You will miss more by not seeing than by not knowing." And that was even before Google!

/ **5.1** / A racehorse groom gave me a great piece of advice when I was young: "Know your horses' legs like the back of your hand, then you'll know when somethin' ain't right."

★ RICE as It Is Relevant to Horses

My best first-aid advice uses the old prescriptive acronym:

1. **R**est—Three days immediately after injury does wonders.
2. **I**ce—Use often, 10 minutes at a time.
3. **C**ompression—Learn how to properly bandage.
4. **E**levation—Good luck!

Taking the time necessary to be careful and thorough is crucial to "seeing."

/ 3 / Finally, utilize integrative diagnostics to enhance what you can see and feel. I use postural analysis, a diagnostic acupuncture point exam, and a mobilization exam on all patients routinely. My motto: *the more information the better.*

In my practice, the "more" information includes horsemanship skills. Horses are often brought to me or referred to me after traditional options have worn thin, so I have to be creative, as in the case of Ripa (name changed to protect the innocent). Ripa was a sometime client of mine—the gelding was a jumper whose owner tended to often switch around between lots of different veterinarians. But the owner was also a friend. And she called me one afternoon as she was pulling out of a local veterinary clinic, with her horse in the trailer behind her. With a tinge of desperation in her voice, she asked, "Would you have time to look at Ripa sometime soon? I am at my wits' end with his lameness right now. We've been treating a ligament tear in his shoulder forever, it seems, but he hasn't gotten any better."

Ripa's owner had caught me at the barn, so I replied, "Sure. Can you head over right now?"

I got the whole story as Ripa was unloaded 15 minutes later and was ambling around the barnyard on a long lead, head down, grazing. Basically, thousands of

/ 5.2 / Dry needling uses sterile, single-use acupuncture needles, placed in one of several hundreds of acupuncture points on the horse's body, to affect the change in the *qi* (life force), which the practitioner desires. I have seen many horses benefit from this therapy.

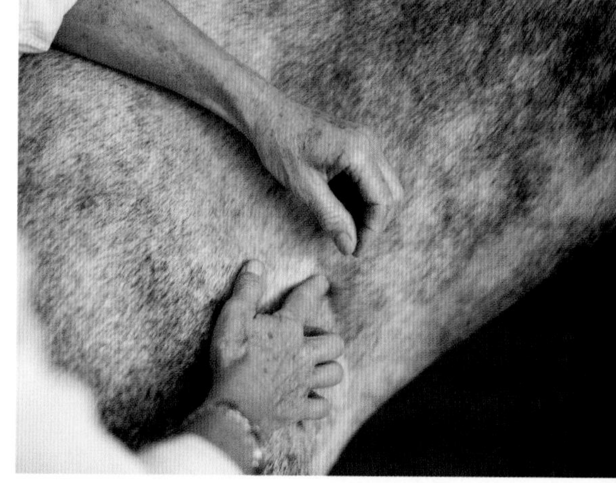

dollars in diagnostics and therapies, and weeks of complying with prescribed rest, hadn't made any difference in the horse's soundness. I performed a diagnostic acupuncture exam, physical exam, and lameness evaluation, and I developed a hunch.

"Would it be okay if I work Ripa in the round pen a little?" I asked.

"Of course," she replied.

I started off nice and easy, just moving him on the rope at the walk and trot in big slow circles. Then I wanted to test his movement off pressure, specifically his shoulders.

What I found confirmed my suspicion: His "unsound" shoulder was super "pushy" and "bossy," while the other one was "yielding" and "compliant." Within a few minutes of playing around with it, however, it became apparent that with pressure, the gelding did move off the "unsound" shoulder better and better. It was a classic "chicken-or-egg" question: Lameness can make a horse protect a side but also innate "sidedness" can appear *like* unsoundness. My bet with Ripa was the latter, and I relayed this to his owner, along with my conclusion that probably his true pain was originating from a sacroiliac (SI) joint. I did some needling and recommended she call the clinic she had just come from and work up the sacroiliac. She did, they injected the SI joint, and the horse went back to full work, sound. A happy ending for all.

I love my round pen.

★ My Favorite Old-Fashioned Horse Care Hack

Place 4-inch by 4-inch gauze sponges in a resealable sandwich container box and fill with hydrogen peroxide. Always have at hand as catching things early is key in treatment. Use topically at first sign of any skin issue as it has good antimicrobial and drying properties without being too caustic. //

Therapies and Treatments

Equine veterinary medicine sometimes benefits from being at the cutting edge of technology. For example, we own one mare, Rio, who was the literal poster girl for stem cell therapy back in 2005. Regenerative therapies are certainly fabulous options. But sometimes it is a detriment to be experimental, such as what happened when the overzealous off-label use of bisphosphonates (drugs that slow bone loss and are believed to reduce the risk of fractures) was causing some lamenesses. There are advantages and disadvantages of being a less regulated field than human medicine. The horse owner needs to be aware of any given situation and speak to her veterinarian about the safety of innovative drugs or technologies before they are employed.

Then there are the centuries-old practices. Acupuncture, for example, still awes me with its power. It's been 25 years since I put my first needle in a horse. The number of needles since are uncountable. But every needling is still done with gratitude and acknowledgment that the horse is

/ 5.3 A & B / Bodywork can release muscular tension, mobilize joints, and fire up neuromuscular pathways **(A)**. Happy horse, happy vet **(B)**.

allowing me to do it. The best tool I have as a veterinarian is acupuncture needles in my hands.

Equine dentistry has gone through a lot of changes (some would say "whiplash") over the last few decades. When power tools first came into vogue in the early nineties, everyone climbed on board, and making a "bit seat" or "performance mouth" in riding horses was all the rage. Now many owners are hesitant to use a veterinarian who uses power tools for dentistry, instead preferring the

old-fashioned, bicep-building rasping methods. It certainly was proven that overuse of power tools can overheat the tooth roots and thus cause damage, but as with many things, the main responsibility lies with the person wielding the tool. Just another example of where innovation has to be tempered with good common sense.

A friend of mine who is an equine masseuse once remarked to me, "I'm shocked at how many sore horses there are out there." I agree and am constantly astounded by how even despite that fact, so many horses keep on performing and trying. Bodywork is essential to finding and addressing these issues. My personal favorite type of bodywork is *Tui Na*, which is a part of traditional Chinese veterinary medicine, and works on the same principles as acupuncture. Watching it done, clients view it as a form of "soft" chiropractic, and it indeed is a way of mobilizing and manipulating the tissues. Horses love it.

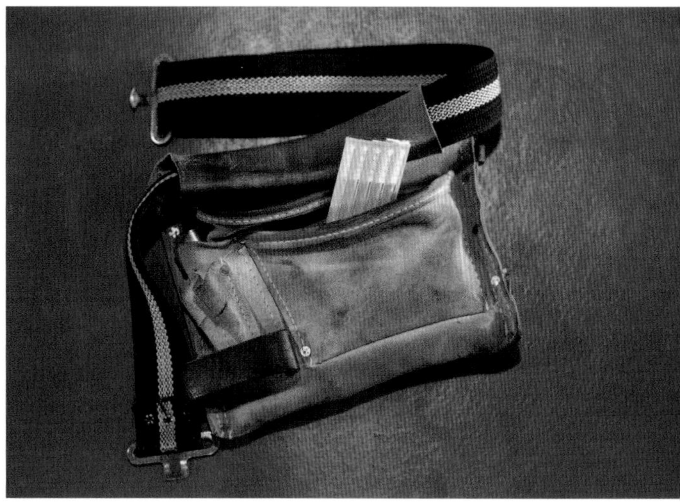

/ **5.4** / A carpenter's belt repurposed as my acupuncture pouch.

Paying Attention

What do a good veterinarian and a good rider have in common? They both have a high degree of ability to pay attention, which derives equally from experience (wisdom) and character (being present and focused).

This presence and focus are primary in the physical care of the horse. I was taught in my acupuncture training to respect a horse's private space—once I enter into the area about a foot or two from the horse's body, I try to stay in there and complete my examination and treatments without making multiple trips back and forth to my vet truck. It makes intuitive sense for my work—I am expressing with my body language that I am present and *with* the horse. (My carpenter's belt allows me to do this, as usually I can fit most of what I need in it.)

I ask permission from the horse to enter his space, either with a "horse handshake" (greeting his nose with my hand) or by pausing just outside his "circle" and letting him adjust to my presence. I also usually keep a hand on my patient at all times, so as to cue

★ Governing Vessel 26

Bell had been standing quietly for my exam and acupuncture needles; however, when I went to insert a hypodermic needle to inject Sarapin into an acupuncture point, he started crow-hopping, then extended his back, raised his head, and kicked out. This was very unusual—very rarely do I ever have a horse act out. He was vulnerable to injury in this position, as was I!

So I decided to (for only the third time in my acupuncture practice, I believe) use a twitch. I put it on, handed it to the experienced groom who was fortunately helping me that day, injected the Sarapin, and had the twitch off in the space of about 10 seconds. Bell stood perfectly quiet for this second attempt.

In some situations, I believe it is safer, quicker, and more humane to place a twitch. A twitch activates an acupuncture point—Governing Vessel 26—that aids in a calming effect. The take-home lesson? Learn how to use a twitch properly (ideally from an experienced horseperson)—it is a great tool to relieve stress for the horse and improve safety for the human, especially for short, potentially challenging procedures. You hopefully won't have to use the skill often, but when you do need it you really need it. //

him as to my whereabouts. And when I do leave his side, I try to remember to make it deliberate, sometimes with a flat hand on his body and backing away, so that he knows that I'm leaving and that he is to stay put.

Petticoat

As an equine veterinarian, I've had my share of really stressful situations—when a 1,000-pound animal is throwing himself around in pain or running crazy from a penicillin reaction, things get "real," real quick. I have always tried to keep my own farm a little calmer than this world that I often saw on rounds. I also really dislike emergencies, so everything I could possibly do in the way of preventive care, I have done. And then eventually I realized that I really preferred that way of thinking—proactive and holistic—and I was fortunate enough to be able to remove the proverbial "siren and lights" from the roof of my vet truck and focus my practice on what came naturally to me.

One particularly fraught experience occurred in my early years of veterinary practice, in our own barn.

"Hey, Shelley," Haley, who worked for Adam in the barn, said over the phone, sounding distraught. "Petticoat pulled back from the wash rack, fell over backward, and now she's got blood trickling down from her nose. What should we do?"

"I'll be right there," I responded.

I ushered my two young sons out of the house and bundled them into the back seat of my veterinary truck, buckling the littlest one into his car seat. I drove to the barn and parked alongside my home-clinic door so I could keep half an eye on my children. I rolled down the windows, and told them to stay in the truck and entertain themselves with the books and toys I kept behind the front seats just for that purpose. There was a polo practice game going on, so the barnyard was buzzing with horses and trailers and people—I knew someone would come find me if the kids needed me.

Petticoat was standing quietly on the wash rack and, indeed, had a small stream of blood flowing from one nostril. She was a chestnut mare we had in training from a friend and supporter of Adam's; I didn't know her that well, but I knew what I was looking at could spell trouble.

I led the mare carefully to the treatment area in front of the clinic. My plan was to start by placing a catheter to allow easy access for sedation, medication, and fluids she would likely require. I got all my supplies ready and prepped the area over Petticoat's left jugular vein, but as I inserted the needle tip, she gave a little head toss. The trickle immediately turned into a torrent. Blood was flowing full-width out of both nostrils, like you'd turned on a garden hose.

Now I knew my foreboding was correct—I was dealing with a carotid artery rupture caused by the trauma to her head. It is life-threatening because horses are obligate nose-breathers (they can't get air through their mouths because of their unique throat anatomy), and if I was going to save this mare's life, I needed to get a tracheotomy in, fast. She was already starting to panic—her eyes were wide and she was pawing—as she realized she was having trouble breathing.

It's hard to remember the exact sequence of the events that happened next. I know I didn't use local anaesthetic—I just ran for a scalpel blade, and I think I got through the first layer of tissue while she was still in the cross-ties. (Thankfully it had been drilled into me in vet school: *cut vertically through the skin and tissue layers, then horizontally between tracheal rings.*) But then Petticoat started losing control, and I somehow got her into the adjacent stall and closed the door as she started going through paroxysms.

I have other vague memories: My older child peering out the car window and worriedly inquiring, "Is everything ok?" (I think I said yes...) Petticoat spraying blood all over the walls of the stall as she repeatedly fell down and got up. One of Adam's teammates who happened to be on his way to the barn bathroom, begging me to stop trying to save her, pleading, "Think of your children!" I do know I came very close to losing the mare. At one point, my improvised "trach tube"—a cut-off syringe cap—was dislodged yet again, and that was when she was almost agonal. She knocked me down in her struggles, but I escaped the stall, crawling on my hands and knees, got back to my feet, and re-entered to get the tube back in place. It was surreal; and it still is, when I think about it now—how absorbed I was; how "in the zone."

Later that evening Petticoat was stable enough for us to ship her to the University of Georgia Veterinary Teaching Hospital, where she was monitored and received fluids, antibiotics, and support for her anemia. It was exceedingly rare to have a horse survive such an event because usually the vet didn't arrive in time. It was lucky that I had been on the farm when the call came in. My clothes covered in blood, I drove home, threw everything I had on in the washing machine, and fixed the kids dinner.

/ 5.5 / The white Bowie 5-drawered veterinary unit in the back of my truck I've worked out of since 1998 feels like an extension of myself… or a trusted partner. It gives me confidence I can handle whatever situation arises (my small human first aid kit in the back of the top-right drawer has come in handy on many occasions as well!)

My neighbor corralled me a few weeks later, ribbing me that I must feel so good every time I looked at Petticoat, munching on hay in her paddock. It did feel good when he mentioned it, but honestly, I preferred to not think about what had happened.

I haven't been able to save them all. I remember one mare that had a catastrophic injury on the polo field. Radiographs revealed a comminuted fracture (which means the bone had shattered into multiple pieces)—a devastatingly poor prognosis. Her owner made the humane decision to put her down. But for the 20 to 30 minutes it took to do the work-up, before any of us knew how bad it was, I didn't leave her side. I braced the mare up, helping her stand without placing weight on her injured leg. I can still feel the weight of her in my back and in my arms, my shoulder pressed against her flank. I can still hear myself talking to her, and see myself stroking her. I think she knew she was being taken care of—however terrifying those last moments might have been—for she was calm. It is a gift you can give to any creature—comfort in the face of pain. And as tough as it is, it is the reason I love my job.

// *Winning Point*

In traditional Chinese veterinary medicine theory, the *qi* that flows through the meridians in animals interacts with the *qi* of the cosmos. You don't have to "believe" that as fact to understand that it is a profoundly different way of looking at the world. Practicing acupuncture for decades has certainly influenced me insofar as I am more aware of the holistic nature of our lives.

Integrative medicine encourages a doctor to see the forest as well as the trees, and this translates to looking for root causes instead of just treating symptoms. I believe this medical philosophy is vital to the ethical continuation of horse sport because otherwise it is all too easy for the horse to be treated as a commodity or as a vehicle to "do his job" of satisfying a rider's ambition, instead of being viewed as a living creature with his own place in this world. //

end *of* chapter 5

CHAPTER

6

Veterinary Decisions While Competing

Moderation means prevention.
Prevention means achieving virtue.

– Lau-tzu –

// Veterinary Decisions While Competing

The innovations that Shelley brought to my stable felt like a competitive edge. She checked every horse after each match, running a plastic syringe cap down their energy meridians to see if any points were reactive; then treated discomfort, either with acupuncture or Western medicine, before it could get worse. Preventive, holistic, creative, individualized—her care was a step way beyond what my peers were doing with their horses. It was a dream scenario, knowing the "horse care" was covered. Even though it was someone else's responsibility (Shelley's), I knew it was being done and done well. So, when I settled into the saddle and entered the field of play, I was confident that every detail had been seen to. The horses were happy and healthy. All I had to do was play.

When spectators see a great horse making it look easy in a tournament finals, it's hard to comprehend just how much consideration and care has gone into these animals' performance. Here are a few horse stories that illustrate the value of proper veterinary care.

CHAPTER 6

When Pumbaa played two chukkers in the 2002 US Open Finals, she was sensational. I scored two goals on her the first time I was on her, in the second chukker, then got the game winner halfway through the sixth, and we set up the goal that put the game away in the final minute. She was big, and gray, and so powerful that she dominated other horses on the field. For her efforts that day, she earned the Hartman Trophy for Best Playing Pony of the US Open. She was nine years old. And it is still the best, single-game performance I have ever ridden. What most spectators did not realize, seeing her draped in a royal blue "BPP" blanket in the winner's circle, was that she had previously sustained a career-threatening bout with Equine Protozoal Myeloencephalitis (EPM), a disease that affects the central nervous system.

There have been many veterinary success stories when it comes to our horses, but Pumbaa's is one of the most poignant. She came to us as an energetic five-year-old. Her owner, Mike Galvan, called me at the end of the 1998 Florida season, and asked if I would come ride his gray mare.

"I think she's got a lot of potential, and I'd like you to take her for the off-season," was his gist.

He wasn't trying to sell her (at least not overtly), he just wanted me to take her to Aiken and play her for a while, because he liked the way I rode.

I went and sat on Pumbaa one afternoon at the Everglades polo field. It was just the two of us out there on a 10-acre pitch. She was a little frisky, and oozed athleticism...*if* it could be channeled in the right direction. And what did I have to lose? So I agreed to take her, with one stipulation: that if I fell in love with her, I would have first option to purchase her for a *reasonable* price. Mike agreed.

That May, Mark Bryan, a trainer working with us at the time, played Pumbaa in her first four-goal game at Aiken Polo Club. And then I played her for two or three weekends in pro-am exhibition matches, which I always found to be a nice step for a young horse before entering them in higher goal, tournament polo. She didn't get rattled in these flowy, white-pants practice matches. And she was obviously fast and athletic, but it still hadn't clicked about just what a talent I was riding.

For our first competitive polo together the following fall, I entered Pumbaa in a 16-goal tournament. I will never forget the feeling from the first 20 seconds or so of stepping onto the field. We were playing at Foxcroft Farm in Alpharetta, Georgia, and the mare was still only five years old. First games on green horses always made me nervous. Neither of us knew what to expect. But I started on Pumbaa in the fourth chukker, in order to give her a good warm-up over halftime, and our first play together was a "knock-in" (bringing the ball in off the end line). The moment I stroked the ball off the backline, I had the overwhelming sensation that nobody could touch us. I tapped the ball a time or two forward and to the right—a conservative knock-in to start the rookie horse—felt her right there underneath me, and then swatted the ball 50 yards sharp left under her neck. She was so quick getting back to the ball that it felt like cheating...and we'd created yards of space. And all the while, I knew that if an opponent got too tight on us, she'd go right by them. It was an incredible feeling—of floating, with an immense power in the control of my hand and legs. I can't even recall the results of that match, but I remember the feeling Pumbaa gave me like it was yesterday. I had never felt anything like it.

The next time I was with Mike Galvan in person was in Aiken, and I invited him to my barn office where we sat and debated the meaning of the word *reasonable*. Eventually we agreed on a price, I wrote him a check, and Pumbaa became part of my string. Her first game in Florida that next winter she helped me score three goals in the sixth chukker of our 22-goal opener, and our team came from behind to win. It was that same floating feeling, but now we were facing elite competition. I remember Frederick Roy, horse lover and the late publisher of *The Morning Line*, coming up to me after the game and exclaiming about Pumbaa in his French accent: "That gray, so exciting! *Incroyable*! Her debut and she's your new champion!"

He was right.

Perhaps it was too good to be true, because that season, that feeling didn't last. When I singled her (rode her alone), she was high as a kite. It felt like sitting on a keg of dynamite. One day, hacking her around the track at South 40, I raised my right hand to wave to a friend passing in a car, and she spun left and bolted. I grabbed leather and managed to hang on by a toe, but I remember thinking, *No more sudden movements while I'm sitting on Pumbaa.* Was it just youthful exuberance?

On the playing field the change was gradual, but into our second tournament she no longer felt like the "new champion" she had at the start of the season. She had gotten more strung-out, not as collected underneath me. And I found myself not trusting her to play in the crunch time (fifth and sixth chukkers). Maybe she was getting tired? I chalked it up to it being her first "real season" in Florida. And I had to remember that she was only six years old.

Then one day Shelley was going through my horses, giving them her "whole horse" vet check between games. Our experienced Brazilian grooms Bento and Bete held the individual horses for her, and Shelley liked to ask about behavioral issues they may have noticed back at the barn or while out on sets. After all, they spent more hours with these horses on a daily basis than anyone else. When Shelley asked about Pumbaa, it turned out that Bete had recently witnessed something *muy raro*. The last time she had roached Pumbaa's mane, Bete had been reaching up to clip between her ears, when the mare stumbled and nearly collapsed in her stall.

"*Casi me mata*," ("Almost killed me,") Bete said with a grimace.

Already Shelley had been considering neurological possibilities for the root cause of the changes in my former rising star—the "tiredness" and "flatness" that I had noticed on the polo field. But with Bete's description of what seemed like dizziness or a loss of motor control, the coin dropped (at least for me). When I thought about it, I *had* noticed Pumbaa rolling over a back foot—a little half-stumble behind—once in a while when easing her around the sand track on one of our "calming" trail rides. I had chalked it up to uneven ground but couldn't recall any other horses stumbling in the same manner, *and* it was a new occurrence since the start of the season. Shelley pulled blood, sent a sample to the lab for testing, and the results came back a strong positive for EPM. This was the first such diagnosis that any of my horses had ever had. It was scary.

And this was where Shelley's expertise and horse sense took over. Her attention to detail is the special ingredient that has allowed for longevity, or, as in the case of Pumbaa, comebacks in the careers of many of my best horses. In these situations, Shelley makes all the calls. And, because I inherently trust her choices, she has total freedom to decide what she thinks is best for the horse. Perhaps Shelley's choices weigh toward the *horse welfare* side of the seesaw, with me leaning in the direction of *next competition*, but it makes for a good balance.

Pumbaa's season was over, but she was in good hands.

There was hope that we had caught the disease early enough, and that with treatment and some luck, Pumbaa could still enjoy a playing career. I recall certain aspects of her rehabilitation. Work was stopped immediately. Stress apparently could be a contributing factor for EPM, and certainly the new routine of Pumbaa's first high-goal polo season could be considered a source of stress. There was an experimental drug, Baycox®, that we specially ordered from Canada and administered orally for 30 days. Then Pumbaa returned to our farm in Aiken where she would, hopefully, "destress" in a field with her pasture mates.

There were a lot of unknowns about EPM back in 1999 (and still are). "A neurological disorder caused by eating possum poop" was basically what I understood it to be. It seemed mysterious, but it was also dangerous, and in some cases even fatal. But unlike a tendon or ligament injury, requiring a certain amount of rest followed by graded reconditioning, there were no specific timetables for a return to competition after EPM treatment (or, at least, the data didn't yet exist). At some point we would learn if our treatment of Baycox and rest had worked to counter the disease fully, partially, or not at all. The most substantial improvements reportedly could be observed within weeks of administering the drug. And, after that, there was only one way to find out.

That summer I was contracted to play the Queens Cup and Gold Cups in England. I hadn't played there since 1994, and it would be my first time playing the UK season on my own horses. The plan was that my team would fly nine of my best horses over in early May, and these horses would return to the States at the end of July. Pumbaa would have had two months' rest, and still some time to be legged up on the farm, and I wanted to bring her. Even if I didn't play her full chukkers, she gave me confidence, and there was no reason she couldn't play as a spare. Shelley okayed the plan.

I'm not sure either of us would have approved the plan had we known how rough a flight it would be. But players flew their horses regularly without incident, and it didn't seem more risky than a multi-day trailer ride to my mind. Plus, if I wanted to play the season in England, this was the transport provided by my team, Mirage. It wasn't like preparing my own trailer for a long haul—all we could do was prepare my string of horses as well as possible (ensure they were rested, fit, and well fed) and hope all went well.

A cargo plane was chartered for transport and refitted with portable, plywood standing stalls to carry 92 horses. There were polo ponies and grooms from three teams on the flight, and Bento and Bete traveled with my horses. The first hiccup was a two-hour delay on the tarmac at Miami International while a glitch in the paperwork was being resolved. The temperature rose above 90 degrees Fahrenheit in the cargo area, and there was no water to drink. Once airborne, it was frigid in the hold, and Bento and Bete spent much of the flight wrapped in extra horse blankets for warmth. Then, roughly halfway through the trip, the aircraft made an unexpected descent. Word filtered back that they were landing in Iceland to refuel. And the landing was a rough one. The aircraft bounced once badly off the runway, sending the horses crashing against partitions as they scrambled to keep their balance, before it eventually settled back down on the landing strip.

Once back in the air, one of our horses, Kanji, began struggling to lie down, but her stall was too narrow to allow it. Bento got in an argument with one of the "horse guards" who wanted to tranquilize her rather than alter the formation of the stalls, but finally Bento was allowed to take one partition from the stall so that Kanji could get down and rest. It was not the smooth trip we would have wished for any of the horses, but eventually they made it across the Atlantic and negotiated a smooth landing at Gatwick Airport, outside London.

Despite the wild flight, Pumbaa did really well that summer in England. At age six, she was the youngest horse in my string, playing only her second high-goal season, and was possibly still recovering from EPM. Since my other horses were older and more experienced, I used Pumbaa mostly as a spare. Maybe it was good for her to only play a couple minutes here and there, not get exhausted from playing a full seven minutes, and it gave me confidence to know I could get on her for short bursts. I remember one play at Guards Polo Club, where she bounced off Argentinian Sebastian Merlos and went for the ball. "Sebi" was screaming for a foul, but there was no whistle. She had just overpowered his horse, the way she could.

After my horses returned to the United States (on what was, fortunately, a less eventful flight) Scott Parker (a professional driver we've been using for years) picked them up from their brief quarantine near Miami International Airport and drove them home to New Haven Farm. They would get three months out on pasture before being legged up for their next Florida season. They deserved it. Shelley treated Pumbaa again with another 30-day course of Baycox. It couldn't hurt, and if it helped to set back the disease a little more, or ideally knock it out, then the money would be well worth it.

Over the next two years, Pumbaa started floating again. She had gained the experience that allowed her to be more settled around the barn and on the playing field. Shelley devised a strategy that I would play her for only parts of the seasons—the last two tournaments of Santa Barbara, or only the 26-goals in Wellington—because we didn't want to deplete her and give the EPM a chance to resurface. Shelley had recently become certified in veterinary acupuncture (receiving her CVA from the International Veterinary Acupuncture Society), and her needles now provided another diagnostic and curative tool to help Pumbaa, and all our horses, stay healthy and performing their best.

In 2001 my team, Templeton, reached the finals of the Gold Cup, the second-most prestigious polo tournament in the United States after the US Open. From the semi-finals, I can still picture Pumbaa exploding by 10-goaler Marcos Heguy to score the winner late in the sixth chukker.

"*Que bestia*!" Marcos fumed afterward. It was meant as a compliment.

In those days the players in the finals were each given two numbered saddle pads for their best playing pony candidates. As I usually did when both ponies

★ Horses I Loved

When I say *I loved* a horse, it means I loved to play him; or, for example, that I would happily enter a sudden-death overtime chukker on him. There were seven horses I loved on my string that summer in England—Hale Bopp, Tequila, Bag Lady, Jill, Josephine, Kanji, and Pumbaa. Usually polo players, including me, just have one or two game-winners that they play in overtime. I still can't believe how fortunate I was to have those seven talented and amazing horses all together at once. //

were competing with me in the finals of a tournament, I picked Hale Bopp and Pumbaa to wear numbers that day. And Hale Bopp, who you will come to know intimately in these pages, was selected BPP of the 2001 Gold Cup. In 2002, however, it was Pumbaa's turn. I was playing #2 for Coca Cola, a position where Pumbaa's power was a huge asset—both for shutting down the best player on the other team and for scoring goals. And after getting nipped by a goal in the finals of the '02 Gold Cup, we knew we had a good team. We weren't practicing our best horses at all between games, since the other three team members were headed to England that summer and wanted to save their horses as much as possible. And this suited me just fine. I've often felt that most polo players over-practice their horses—either for something to do, out of fear of their horses being "heavy," or to avoid riding singles. And with 15 teams in the '02 US Open, there would be no shortage of games.

★ BPPs

It was always tough for me selecting just two horses as best playing pony (BPP) candidates, because as any equestrian can tell you, it can be difficult to know which horse will shine on any given day. And I made a couple mistakes. After winning the Pacific Coast Open in 2005, I was told that "the brown mare in the fourth would have won hands down" had I put a number on her. Sorry, Bag Lady. But the practice of making players choose two prior to a match made the judges' job easier, since they then only had to watch those horses wearing the specified numbers. And, I always appreciated learning which horses my competitors felt were the best in their strings. //

The afternoon before each match we usually rode singles on the team's Everglades field (coincidentally the same place I had first tried Pumbaa). I had a rough pattern I followed: a loping warm-up twice around the 10-acre polo field, once on each lead; some different-sized circles at varying speeds; my "railroad tracks," where you turn tight and try to come out parallel to the track you came in on; half-circles with full stops (just two) and rollbacks in both directions; a field-length gallop with slaloming flying lead changes; and a quiet halt with a soft back-up for a step or two. And then on to the next one. I loved riding Pumbaa

/ 6.1 / With Pumbaa, the gray blur, scoring the go-ahead goal of the 2002 US Open in the sixth chukker. She won the best playing pony prize that day.

over this imaginary course. We were relaxed, this was easy, and she glided effortlessly through her exercises. When we stopped and rolled, it was like she curled up underneath me, rocking her weight back, bringing her front legs across, and propelling us forward with her hindquarters in any direction my eyes were looking. She felt like silk, and I could ride that feeling all day!

In our six games (all wins) leading up to the US Open finals, I played either eight or nine horses. Six different horses would start chukkers, and two or three would be used as spares. In the week leading up to the finals, I phoned Shelley (who had returned to Aiken after the tournament's semi-finals to manage our children's school commitments) to ask about doubling (riding in two chukkers) Hale Bopp and Pumbaa.

"I thought the same thing," she responded.

This was music to my ears. Shelley wanted what was best for our horses but also valued the competitive goals that were linked to their performance. *These two things could be aligned.* She recognized a once-in-a-lifetime opportunity, and like me, she wanted to win. But she had given me the peace of mind to double my best two horses, worry-free; not only because of her affirmation of my plan, but because of her attitude—now part of our program—of providing these horses with everything they needed all along the way.

Pumbaa soared that day—she was a gray, bottomless, blur—largely due to the care and rehabilitation that Shelley had provided behind the scenes.

Hale Bopp: When Age Comes Calling

About halfway through my 2009 Florida high-goal season, Hale Bopp came up lame. At the time she was 17. Our team's veterinarian assessed her, found degenerative changes in one front ankle, suggested injecting that joint with hyaluronic acid and cortisone, and said she'd be ready to go for our next game in three days' time.

"Don't I have to give her two to three days of stall rest after a joint injection?" I asked.

"That's what some do, but I must have injected..." he made a gesture with his hand that indicated countless numbers (that return to work right away) "...and no problems."

That should have been a red flag.

Shelley was in Aiken with our three kids, as well as the "turnouts"—she had enough on her plate. I felt it was unfair to ask her advice if she couldn't put her hands or eyes on the mare.

Hale Bopp had hardly missed a chukker since she came to me over a decade before as a sprightly six-year-old. But what could I expect, with the number of games she had played for me over the years, and her age? There weren't many, if any, late "teenagers" playing in the US Open. And maybe the injection would help her feel better. And this veterinarian *did* have years of practical experience—all over the polo world, in fact. Couldn't I trust that?

And I really wanted to play Hale Bopp in our next game.

The beginning of the season had been tough. I was 45 years old, about to turn

★ MVPs

We did find a way to turn the season around and ended up making it through to the finals of the US Open, a match we lost in sudden death overtime to a very strong Audi team. My teammate Eduardo Novillo Astrada and I shared MVP honors. It is rare for a member(s) of the losing team to win MVP, and it remains the only time in the history of the sport that the Seymour H. Knox Award has been shared. //

46, and it was the first time I noticed myself sometimes getting "out-quicked" on the field. After one loss, I even admitted this sensation to my teammates. It was an upsetting realization, but it helped to voice it. And I had to live with the reality that I was getting old(er).

"In season," like at that moment with Hale Bopp, I pretty much only thought about my next game. The mare may no longer have been the fourth chukker dynamo who I could bring back for overtime—she'd naturally lost a step or two—but she still turned like a top, and more than anything, she gave me confidence. I was starting her in the first chukker of most matches.

And, on her, I still felt quick out there.

So my relief at hearing the team veterinarian tell me she could play buried my concerns about safe protocol. And I said yes to the injection.

That afternoon the team veterinarian administered the intra-articular dose of hyaluronic acid and cortisone. The ankle was wrapped and Hale Bopp rested that night in her stall as usual. The next morning she went on a walk set, and a light trot, with her normal group of horses—her "friends." And that afternoon the ankle had additional swelling and heat. There was an attempt to treat the "flare" with injectable antibiotics; her return to work was halted.

Shelley arrived from Aiken for a pre-scheduled visit, took one look at our mare and said, "We have to get her to a hospital as soon as possible."

Shelley was afraid the joint had gone septic.

I remember loading her onto our trailer—one horse alone in a space big enough for 12—and driving her to Dr. Byron Reid's urgent care facility back among the canals in Loxahatchee, Florida. She stayed for five days, underwent surgery, had her ankle lavaged multiple times, and for the first 36 hours there was some question about whether she would survive.

I hated myself for putting Hale Bopp in the situation she was in. Visiting her each day—seeing her alone and confused, in a strange place, and obviously in a lot of pain—made me cry. I began to truly question what I was doing. I wondered whether high-level competition, and the pressures and demands on this horse, and other horses, were truly worth it. Honestly, at that moment, I would have given all my successes back to save Hale Bopp.

Writing these words, even now, I feel a pit in my stomach. For *what* had I put her in that situation? So I could continue playing a 17-year-old mare who had given me her heart and soul for eleven years? It was worse than that, because I had agreed to overlook safety protocols, with the short-term interest of not missing even one game on her blinding me to what I knew to be right. I couldn't blame the veterinarian. He had been hired by the team, and helping our team win short-term was his primary aim. Injecting the joint may have been his suggestion, but it was my decision. An owner is ultimately responsible for the welfare of his horse. In this case my "next game selfishness" had a huge cost, because it meant the end of my favorite mare's playing career. And when I saw her in the hospital, I would gladly have given up ever being able to play her again, if it meant I could take back my mistake. My prayer was simply that Hale Bopp would have the ability to live contentedly again with her friends for the rest of her days. It put things in perspective when her life was on the line.

There had been one other occasion when we thought Hale Bopp's life was in jeopardy. But that time had been on the playing field, where accidents can happen. At the time she was eight or nine years old and we were playing the Sunday, 3:00 pm game at Palm Beach Polo and Country Club.

There was a quick change of direction in front of the stands, and Hale Bopp turned so fast that an opponent caught us from behind, and we went down in a heap. When I picked myself up off the ground, the first thing I saw was my mare standing on three legs, holding one foreleg in the air like it was broken. The next thing I saw was my groom, Bento, who must have raced out from the sidelines upon seeing the wreck. But then I noticed that he was wielding one of my spare mallets like a club and demanding, "*Quien fue*?" ("Who was it?") Thankfully, nobody dared tell him who had hit us because he looked ready to take matters into his own hands. Shelley was out there, too, and that was a huge relief. Not only was she a veterinarian who loved this mare as much as I did, but she was calm in a crisis.

The emergency van drove out, we stripped Hale Bopp's tack, found a halter, and Shelley led our mare, hopping,

★ The Sunday Match

Almost all major polo tournament finals are played at 3:00 pm on Sundays. Since tournaments typically last anywhere from two weeks to a whole month, and the host club features a match for the crowd (and corporate sponsors) each Sunday, sometimes your team draws this "stadium venue." It is significant only because there is a little extra excitement with the crowd and the announcer, and possibly an MVP award. In the wreck I had with Hale Bopp, we went down on the side of the field nearest the main grandstand. //

★ Consider Trailer Noise

Like Shelley, I experienced the racket of the trailer while riding in back—in my case while accompanying a mare and foal. I could understand all the rattling on our dirt road, but what I wasn't prepared for was the noise that continued—only slightly abated—once we hit pavement. Since our personal experiences, we have taped the gate pins, affixed rubber stoppers, and made sure to oil all the hinges...but it's still loud. I have considered putting ear plugs (or sound hoods) on the horses for long trips to try to ease any stress the noise might cause, but I have yet to try it. //

three-legged, up the ramp of the trailer. Shelley rode in back with Hale Bopp to provide some comfort on the short trip to the Palm Beach Equine Clinic. Of that ride Shelley remembers two things: the cacophony of riding in the back of an aluminum gooseneck trailer (every bump made all the moving parts rattle) and observing Hale Bopp as she began to gradually bear weight again on her front leg. By the time they reached the clinic and Hale Bopp was unloaded, the mare was barely limping. The radiographs were negative—no fractures. And when Bento showed up in my rig after the match, Hale Bopp climbed on board, sound as a bell, to rejoin her friends and her routine. She had been badly "stung" in the accident, but we had dodged a bullet.

Back in Loxahatchee at Dr. Reid's hospital, Hale Bopp's situation gradually improved. Of course it would—she was nothing if not a fighter. By the end of the week, I was able to trailer her back to our barn. She was wounded and lame, but the infection had been beaten. And my prayer had been answered: she would be able to live out her days on pasture at our farm.

There were big offers to buy her as a broodmare. We were asked to ship her to Argentina where they could take embryos and mass produce as many little Hale Bopps as possible. But even though we were offered half her progeny, my moral compass (Shelley) wouldn't let me even consider it. We (I) owed Hale Bopp the best home I could give her for the remainder of her years. And, *if* we ever decided to breed her, it would be as natural a process as possible.

/ 6.2 A & B / Hale Bopp in action on the right **(A)**. She was always a thrilling horse to watch play. And with her groom, Bento, waiting to receive a BPP prize after a 20-goal finals in Santa Barbara, California **(B)**.

For eleven more years she lived contentedly on our farm. Her playing days were over, but gradually her ankle got better. And it was a joy to watch her short-strided burst of speed as she galloped toward the gate to ambush her feeder. If it was me, I usually took time to stroke her coat or rub her back for a bit while she tossed Equine Senior and beet pulp from her bin to the ground. And each time I laid my hands on her, all those memories of our playing days together came rushing back.

/ 6.3 / Tequila, in the foreground, showing off her strength and propulsive power.

Tequila: The Doubt Inspired by Injury

"Next time you're at the barn, go into her stall with a calm mind, run your hand down that leg, and feel what's going on. Let her tell you."

As I recall, these were Shelley's words of advice over the phone back in August of 2000. The best horse of that season, Tequila, had come up with a bump on her tendon after the semi-finals, and I was faced with the decision of whether to play her in the finals of the Pacific Coast Open three days later. An experienced local vet had assessed the injury and okayed her to play.

Shelley usually made these calls, balancing my competitive goals with the long-term health interests of our horses. Repeatedly, she got these equations right—to the point where I stopped worrying about them. If she said a horse couldn't play, no problem, I would do the best I could on the horses that were healthy. And if she gave the green light, I trusted the decision and played those minutes all-out. Her skill and comprehension and ethics were a luxury that allowed me to play free.

But, Shelley was not with me in California. She had flown home to get our oldest son back for school.

2

Even after ice and NSAID treatment, Tequila's leg retained a degree of heat and swelling. Not a lot, or it wouldn't have been a difficult call. But enough to present a concern.

And this time it was my call.

Balanced, powerful and cat-quick to both sides, Tequila had become my MVP that season. The feeling she gave was of riding a low-slung jet (perhaps a pod racer) that banked and curved wherever you wanted to go. All season I had played her in the critical fifth or sixth chukker, and I knew there were matches our team would not have won without her.

I entered her stall, fondled her distinctively long ears, and tried to take a quieting breath. Then I bent down beside her left fore, picked up her foot, and palpated her tendon.

"How's it goin' girl?"

Nothing upsets me more than errors of human judgment, made back at the barn, that end up harming our horses. Fortunately, there have not been many—I think I can count them on one hand—but even one is too many, and all of them still hurt. Shelley considers her job to do everything possible to set up our horses for success. With *success* being defined as a combination of high performance (helping a horse fulfill his competitive potential), health, and longevity. On the playing field, I accept that accidents happen; it is a fact of life, in human as well as equestrian sports. But when it comes to decisions made away from the playing field, with the benefit of a calm mind and consultation, well, it feels like there's no excuse for not getting these right. After all, these horses are my responsibility.

Two days after I knelt to feel her leg (Tequila had whispered back that she thought she was okay), I started on her in the sixth chukker of the 2000 Pacific Coast Open finals. We entered that final chukker (seven minutes in length) leading by two, gave up three unanswered goals, and lost the game by a goal. A heartbreaker! Tequila played well. It wasn't her fault. And the next morning at the barn I was relieved to find her leg the same, or even better, than it had been prior to the match.

But what I now know was in my head, lurking for the entire seven minutes that I played her, was doubt. I did not want Tequila to break down because I had made the wrong decision. I had thought she was okay, or else I wouldn't have played her, but who wasn't okay was me. I knew how badly I wanted to win that tournament. I knew—or thought I did—how important Tequila was toward this goal. And I worried that my decision-making had been skewed by my yearning to win. Ultimately, *I couldn't trust myself in making that call*. And, therefore, I played concerned for my horse and about my decision, rather than free.

Tequila's lesson was that I'm better playing all-out on a very good horse than playing concerned on my favorite. And it also impressed upon me the competitive advantage (not to mention the health benefits) that the "tough calls" I routinely expect Shelley to make have meant for me and my horses throughout my career.

There are many factors that ensure riders can ask big questions of their horses without taking everything. In the moment, it might relate to the *feel* of the horse for how much you can push him through the final phase of competition. But it also pertains to the conditioning, maintenance, and long-term management that happens back at the barn. Sadly, some horse owners view a veterinarian's visit with trepidation or gloom because they anticipate a prognosis that will serve to scratch their horse from competition. I'm extremely fortunate to have Shelley in my camp, but it's not necessary to be married to a veterinarian to develop a partnership around the longevity and welfare of your horses. In fact, Shelley tells me that she, as well as most of her peers, would prefer to consult on a regular, preventive basis rather than be called in as a last resort at the eleventh hour.

Although I once saw it as a balancing act between long-term health and short-term goals, it is increasingly apparent that the answer is simple: the long-term wellness of the horse comes first. Even in the case of Tequila, where I chose to take a calculated risk for immediate personal goals, I couldn't achieve those goals because her risk of injury weighed so heavily on my mind. Shelley's influence has steered me toward equine welfare and career longevity, but it also allowed me to be more competitive.

Any athlete would aspire to a long, healthy, relatively pain-free career. Sometimes it takes moderation and forethought to achieve this end with our equine partners. //

end *of* chapter 6

CHAPTER

7

Therapeutic Alternatives

Motion is lotion.

// Therapeutic Alternatives

My unpopular opinion: there has been too much emphasis for too many years in equine sports medicine on developing sophisticated diagnostic techniques that sometimes have no relevance to actually improving horses' lives. This is "unpopular" not only because it flies in the face of scientific "advancement," but also because those expensive machines drive profits. For the average horse owner without medical insurance for their horse, most of the newest procedures are financially out of reach. And even for the ones who *can* afford it, I always ask the questions: "Why are we doing it?" "Will it change what we do for treatment?" "Will it help the horse *get better*?" All too often the answers to these questions are not what you would think they should be—at least from the veterinarian's perspective. We are doing it because the machine is there, and we need to use it to pay it off. The results will make no measurable difference in the way we treat the problem. Gaining the information from the machine or test will not help the horse get better.

CHAPTER 7

/ 7.1 / Bento DaSilva, Adam's long-term groom, warming up Hale Bopp before her chukker. He always rode the polo ponies slowly for a few minutes before they went out onto the field.

Rehabilitation, thankfully, is the newest buzzword in the barn. At long last, I say! Research into methodology and protocols are becoming front and center in veterinary practice. This is innovation that is affordable, catered to address the roots of an individual's problem, and scientifically proven to get results. Although working one-on-one with a qualified practitioner is ideal, here are some concepts and ideas that can get anyone started.

Muscle Health

Horses' muscles allow them to do what humans require—whether that be pull a carriage or carry a rider. Muscle health is thus of primary importance for the successful equine athlete.

Four muscle-specific concepts to differentiate are:

/ **1** / Warm-up

/ **2** / Activation

/ **3** / Cool-down

/ **4** / Stretching

When a sound horse is going to be asked to do movements that come pretty naturally to him (for example, walk, trot, canter), then a warm-up is often all that is needed prior to beginning the task. Most performance situations, however (think polo match, jump course, dressage test, reining pattern), require some combination of the four.

/ **1** / ***Warm-up*** is best described as actually raising the temperature of the muscles in order to optimize their function (which is to *stretch* and *contract*). Thus, the ambient temperature is of prime consideration in deciding how long to stay in this phase. Also important is the housing of the individual—a horse coming in from a 10-acre pasture needs significantly less warm-up than a horse who has been standing in a stall for hours. Another barometer can be *your* warm-up—what do you as a rider need to do before you can sit the trot or execute a reining maneuver? It is likely your horse needs the same consideration!

/ 2 / ***Activation*** of muscles is defined as asking a specific muscle to contract in a specific manner. This is required, in addition to warm-up, if you are asking your horse to do something difficult or "unnatural" for him—such as jumping, passage, or roping a cow. Putting in the time on each ride to get the proper muscles firing before the complicated movement is expected goes a long way toward maintaining soundness. In reality this often means just starting a task at an easier level (jumping low jumps before jumping higher ones, or making small turns before you ask for a roll-back or a pirouette). But it can also be a goal in and of itself—cavalletti work is a good example of a way to activate core muscles. *Core strength* in horses, as in humans, is responsible for the coordination and balance that defines an elite athlete, as well as reducing the chance of injury. Other ways to

★ Say "No" to Carrot Stretches

Warming up muscles before asking them to do anything is crucial to preventing injury—including and especially *stretching*. A pet peeve of mine is so-called "carrot stretches." I believe many people are taught to do them improperly and perform them regularly without thinking of the consequences: The horse may whip his head around, overeager for the treat, and actually hurt himself; he will get into "excitement mode"; he will not really be paying attention to the owner. It comes back to the adage Adam learned from Hector Barrantes in Argentina: *Always have a reason for what you are doing.* Imagine you could formulate the perfect answer if someone who knew nothing about horses asked you, "Why are you doing it that way?" I counsel my clients to only do these types of stretches after riding, when you can rest assured that the horse is warmed up. And I also make sure that the owner varies the exercises—for example sometimes just lowering the head and not going side to side—so the experience is an interaction, not just an unthinking response. //

modify muscle patterns include exercising the horse on varied terrain and surfaces, navigating hills and drops, and incorporating lateral movements into your groundwork and rides.

/ 3 / ***Cool-down*** is important when the horse has exercised vigorously enough to produce lactic acid. This generally only happens if horses are worked at speed or at maximal power. The best way to help clear the accumulated lactic acid is slow jogging for several minutes or until the heart rate starts slowing down, followed by walking until the horse's respiratory rate is normalized.

/ 4 / ***Stretching*** after exercise is optimal—and I know from experience very hard to get into the habit of doing! Any stretching exercises your veterinarian suggests for your horse are most safely performed and most efficacious post-workout (as it is with humans!) so that you can ensure the muscles are already warm. Each stretch should be held for 30 to 60 seconds in order to have the desired effect of *extending muscle length*. If holding one of your horse's rear legs forward toward the ipsilateral (same side) knee for this long sounds like it may be too difficult on your body, you can use a farrier stand.

★ Owning Up

I am guilty of sometimes riding when I probably should be doing therapy on my horse instead. There is never enough time, it seems, and I love to be astride, and I must admit sometimes I don't want to "work" during "my time." But I can always feel how my horses benefit from bodywork, so I try to plan physical therapy ahead of time and then stick to the schedule. //

Physical Therapy

Physical therapy in the horse is best defined as exercises that promote

★ The Shape of the Spine

A simple biomechanical concept to remember regarding horse anatomy is that to best counteract the weight we (unnaturally) load on their backs by riding them, the horse's spine needs to be either *neutral* or in *flexion*. Development of the back and core muscles to maintain this proper position takes time and training, whether from the ground or mounted. A *neutral spine*, provided it is healthy, is perfectly adequate for natural movement. Looking at the horse from the side, this would be how the horse would stand normally. For more efficient under-saddle work, and certainly for collection, jumping, and stopping (think the reining horse sliding to a stop) the back moves into *flexion* to allow for more weight to be shifted to the powerhouse of the hindquarters. Looking at him from the side, the horse's back would appear "lifted." If a horse's spine is in *extension* (looking from the side, there is a dip behind the withers, for example), it disables the power of the hindquarters, and especially if ridden, exposes the horse's back muscles to injury. //

mobilization of joints, strengthening of muscle groups, and increased control and knowledge of how to move. It can be *rehabilitative*, such as after an injury, or *proactive*, to prevent problems from arising in the first place.

One caveat here: recommendations are best given by an experienced practitioner after consulting with your horse in person—"cookie-cutter ideas" are not always that helpful. Some therapy tools have become commonplace in barns—foam pads, shakers, leg weights, resistance band systems, and even aquatic treadmills—but I caution all horsepeople to research the pros and cons of any device, get professional advice, and err on the side of caution in not overusing any particular modality. For example, *swimming* horses has gone in and out of favor over the years because while it is good for soft-tissue injuries and building cardiovascular fitness, it is contraindicated for horses with any axial spine issues (poll, neck, back, sacro-iliac) because of the inverted position it puts horses in. It also exaggerates hind limb motion in an unnatural way while failing to stimulate bone to adapt as concussive forces normally do. Thus, as I see it, swimming is another example of only being helpful if your goals are pinpointed.

Old-fashioned *cavalletti* and *backing up* are my personal favorite forms of physical therapy. They can both be done from the ground or ridden, are easily accessible, and are a very simple and effective tool to tilt the pelvis and engage core muscles. They are also very low risk. And don't forget the huge advantages of simply using different terrains and surfaces. Natural mountain trails with stream crossings are ideal, although few of us have easy access to that! But even shifting from grass to asphalt to dirt to sand helps the horse's proprioception. One concept to remember: *we build stability through challenges to balance.*

I often teach my clients a few simple manual therapy exercises to do with their horses if they are interested. Acupressure combined with various "lifts" and "holds" can be extremely beneficial to patients when targeted toward the deficiencies they have and if taught and executed properly. If you don't have direct access to a veterinarian trained in these kinds of modalities and are interested in learning, there are many great resources available in book and video form. (I highly recommend Jack Meagher's trigger point therapy, Linda Tellington-Jones' TTouch, and Jim Masterson's Masterson Method.)

It can really help if at the beginning of a session with your horse—whether grooming him in the aisle, performing groundwork on a rope, or executing ridden exercises—that you clearly delineate what your goals for the day are. For example, if you know your horse has a tight neck or back, you may want to devote two days a week to just doing physical therapy (on the ground or under saddle), which will make the other days you work with your horse so much more productive. You may want to plan on doing stretches on the days after harder workouts (make a schedule so you stick to it!). If your horse is recovering from injury you may need to spend the extra time going through the entire manual therapy, warm-up, activation, and physical therapy routine every time you ride. It helps to have a plan so you have a reason for what you are doing.

Keep it foremost in your mind how warm-up, activation, cool-down, stretching, physical therapy, and manual therapy (as discussed in chapter 5, p. 67) are distinguished from "training" (by which I mean the inclusion of a mental aspect to the time with your horse). It can smooth out a lot of bumps in the road when you iron out a horse's physical problems separately, and first. The biggest side effect of this work is also a benefit—a more relaxed horse. And as we know, a relaxed horse is a better learner from, a safer companion with, and a better performer for, humans.

// Winning Point

Understanding and applying these modalities are some of the best preventive measures I know. They also help a rider be more in tune with her horse. And as we know, better understanding leads to better results in the competitive arena. //

end *of* chapter 7

CHAPTER

8

Preparing for Competition

Excellence is not a single act, it's a habit.

– Aristotle –

// Preparing for Competition

Don't Look at the Scoreboard

I could fill pages with self-prescribed performance cues:

> *Easy power = loose and send, water method, play the ball with a quiet mind, eyes in, occupy the ball when the opportunity presents, and then look well at the ball and send it to my spot*
>
> *Finish plays = "make some goals out there, Daddy," execute, senses in and go for my moments, breathe, look and go, trust and play*

Some, like *Indonesia*, *Siddhartha smile*, and, *"Okay, next play,"* would require explanation, but the point is that these are the types of things I focused on going into matches. These phrases were pulled from my most recent pregame journal notes. And the *easy power* and *finish plays* cues would have been penned on index cards and tucked into my equipment bag for

CHAPTER

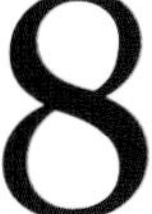

/ **8.1** / Hale Bopp competed all-in, all the time, the way I aspired to play. Here she goes into a huge "bump," against a larger horse, to save a goal in the 2002 US Open Finals. (We got spun sideways, but she kept her feet.)

a particular match. Normally, I glanced at my cue card between chukkers and tried to take a couple calming breaths, but I could also get swept up in the game and forget. Either way was fine. The scripted cues typically changed game to game. But sometimes, when things were going well, I got superstitious and kept the same ones for several matches in a row.

But why is the mental state of the human so important to a sport commonly calculated as 80 percent horse? Because just as horses feel fear, tension, and anxiety, so too do they feel a confident rider with clear intent. The rider's state of mind transfers to the horse. Being present and calm, staying with your breath, and having a positive attitude about your objectives gives your horse an advantage. As Shelley referenced earlier in these pages, one of Olympic eventer Karen O'Connor's key ingredients for effective communication—"a lack of negative emotions"—is implicitly conveyed through an athlete's mental preparation and clarity.

Regardless of which horse sport you compete in, *winning* is the preferred goal. But it is nowhere in my own preparatory thoughts. In fact, the less I think about results, the better I can play. If result-oriented expectations do arise pre-competition, I enjoy the good ones, let the not-so-good ones slip away, and trust that when I begin playing all expectations will disappear. I feel calmest in preparation when I am working with my horses. The thing is to *detach* from the outcome of a match, and thereby free yourself to focus on the "playing" rather than the "winning." For me it's better to not look at the scoreboard.

Tennis great Billie Jean King said that "winning isn't that big a deal. The real joy comes from the very thing that involves people in the first place...the fun of execution, the fun of playing" (*Thinking Body, Dancing Mind*, Bantam, 1994). Don't get me wrong, I always cared deeply about winning. Still do. But I realized that the best chance of achieving my preferred

Orchard
2

result was to put those thoughts away until after the final bell. The goal was to put all my senses into the *here* and *now*, one-play-at-a-time, for as long as it took. So, focusing on what Billie Jean calls the "real joy" of playing also maximizes my chances for the "W" I crave. That's a win-win situation.

I didn't stumble upon these ideas on my own. In 1997, I was interviewed (along with other polo players) by Stiliani "Ani" Chroni, at the time a doctoral candidate from the University of Virginia, writing her dissertation on "Competitiveness in the Sport of Polo." I listened to the questions she posed, we discussed some of my answers, and then I asked if she would work with me. And that was how I began working with a sport psychologist. For 17 years, Ani provided mental coaching services for me and all of the teams I played for, and she still consults informally with me to this day. Our work included yearly in-person marathon sessions, discussing performance issues for four to six hours each day, and lots of phone, fax, and email communication. She favored the Socratic method of questioning and assigned ample amounts of homework to stimulate critical thinking. It was fitting that, in 2016, Ani wrote the foreword for Shelley's and my first book *Polo Life*. She knew us well, had been a participant in many of the events described therein, and presented a perspective that could appreciate the larger picture of family and future, as well as the minutiae of our polo lives.

Ani viewed her task as helping me develop what she called *an unbeatable mind*. This didn't mean that I wouldn't

★ Out of Your Control

For equestrian competitions like reining, cutting, barrel racing, jumping, dressage, eventing, endurance, and working equitation, some examples of *things out of our control* include: the arena footing, a judge's predilections, the course layout, length of the grass, the weather, who's watching, the time slot or draw, static over the PA system, congestion in the warm-up area, the glare of the sun, a barking dog, how your competitors look, and even your coach's final words of advice. //

★ Focus on You, Not Them

The "other team" and "other players" long occupied a large part of my pre-game focus and concern, prior to working with Ani. I thought I was preparing and strategizing, when really I was worrying and speculating. The solution, devised by Ani, was to assess the opponent's strengths and weaknesses two nights before a match, as well as my own team's strengths only. This I did with a few sentences in my journal, and it became my "night before the night before" routine. It was an important part of my preparation. Since I was usually the highest-rated player, I was also acting as captain and on-field coach for many of these teams. But closer to game time, it was more about me, my horses, and my own objectives, and a couple of cue words which I wrote on my index card and stuffed into my game bag. //

lose games, or that opponents wouldn't sometimes beat me and my horses on the field. It meant they couldn't beat *my way of thinking*—that I could maintain my drive, composure, focus, trust, and confidence even while dealing with *force majeure*. Much discussion was centered around what this mindset looked and felt like to me. But we didn't start there.

In and Out of Our Control

Early on, Ani advised me to differentiate between those things *in* and *out* of my control. To this end, theologian Reinhold Niebuhr's "Serenity Prayer" became a sort of mantra:

Grant me the Serenity
to accept the things I cannot change,
Courage to change the things I can,
And wisdom to know the difference.

I found this concept invaluable for minimizing pre-competition distractions. I had to admit that the other team's horses and players, as well as their performances, were out of my control. Indeed, even my own teammates' play, and certainly their horses, were things largely out of my control. So why worry about them?

It simplified my preparation prior to competition to understand that it was really just about me—my horses, my mallets, my play—and that these things were in my hands. Basically, if I took care of everything on my end, gave my horses topnotch care and a perfect prep, then I could *let go, play,* and let the results take care of themselves.

There are obviously many things *within our control* for which we need to take full responsibility. This is essentially our *preparation*. For the rider, this means taking care of our bodies and minds. Exercise, sleep, nutrition, meditation, walking the field, arena, or course, picking a still-point (mine is a tree) at the competition site, visualizing a desired performance, having a plan for distraction control, and remembering to *breathe* are all important elements of my pregame thoughts.

Training and Trusting

Another distinction Ani helped me to recognize—echoing thoughts from my chapter on horse training (p. 45)—is the difference between a *training mindset* and a *trusting mindset*. These factors apply to both equine and human athletes.

Renowned sport psychologist Dr. Bob Rotella wrote about this concept in *Golf Is Not a Game of Perfect* (Simon & Schuster, 1995), specifically in chapter 3: "Train It and Trust It." A *training mindset* implies work, practice, a progression of skills, thinking about what you're doing, and questioning in order to discover what works best in terms of mechanics. The trusting mindset is about *play*. Here, an athlete does not think too much; she sees and responds to the situation at hand, is positive and present. This trusting mindset invokes confidence, for which my favorite definition is

★ Positive Thoughts

I recently heard one coach's instructions just before her student entered the ring for the stadium jumping phase of a three-day event: "Don't make the mistakes you always do." I couldn't believe my ears! To my way of thinking, there could be no worse mindset with which to enter the competitive arena. First, the rider should be focused on where she wants to go—like a mountain biker negotiating a narrow path who stays laser focused on the track he wishes to maintain, and not the pitfalls that lie to either side. And then, the coach had provided a negative distraction at the very moment when horse and rider needed to trust their preparation and instincts. I say *fake it until you make it!* Send yourself out to compete with a positive thought in mind! //

★ Look and Go

I went to the Augusta Quarter Horse Futurity to watch the cutting competition. When a horse-and-rider pair got a particular steer separated from the pack, it looked like the horse got low and went into an autopilot mode, scooching back and forth with his belly inches from the dirt, keeping that cow well back of the herd. The riders were just staying centrally balanced, letting their horses be free to do their job—to *look* and *go*. //

”

Just as a golfer must train his swing and then trust it, a rider must train her horse and then trust him.

Bob Rotella's: *Confidence is playing with your eyes*. The idea is to look forward to every next play/jump/movement instead of hanging on to the previous one. Toward this end, I devised the phrase, "Okay, next play," something that became part of my self-talk on the field, and which I whispered over and over again during matches. As Dr. Rotella stated: *a golfer must train his swing and then trust it.* The same is true for our combination with our horse. No matter the discipline, there comes a point when rider and horse have done everything possible to prepare together for competition. When it comes to our riding, now it is time to shut off our thinking, and to *look* and *go*.

One email I recently came across included a summary of a particularly tough season in Santa Barbara, California. I was 46 at the time, still playing high-level polo, but the team hadn't gelled, and I was frustrated that some of my skills had begun to decline. Here is Ani's response identifying some of the key concepts of a *playing mind:*

(8/29/10) *Little things and bigger things may happen, some of them may even appear as distractions for a short period of time, but your playing mind is well-trained and* ***quietness*** *and* ***trust*** *are the key concepts. You always know what to do, sometimes things go easier than other times. Yet you are always there, on the field with all your strengths, instincts, and experiences. You know to expect setbacks, it's a ballgame played with eight loose cannons! Expect great plays and messes, wins and losses, they are part of the games. Don't expect that everything will go as* *planned, that is why you've gotten so good at being adaptable through your playing years. Expect from yourself to go onto the field with a quiet mind and a jittery stomach, a game plan, and then expect no more. Go in, look and respond, no thinking, no wondering, no questioning...just playing; pass, shoot, ride, mark with determination and faith. Keep your head up at all times, this is polo!!!* (Stiliani Chroni PhD, Sports Psychologist)

Ani is not a horse person. In fact, I can't remember ever having seen her on a horse. But I don't think it's any coincidence that both *trust* and *quietness*—what she identifies as the key concepts of my playing mind—are, also, fundamentally linked to good riding. With the horse, the *trust* is based on experience, practice, and then our own belief in that foundation. There is confidence in that *trust*, positivity. Similarly, *quietness* with our horse is both physical, in terms of our seat and hands, as well as the mental state (contagious) which we bring to the equation. If we approach this interaction with a quiet mind and convey a sense of calm and patience (just as Shelley describes in chapter 5—p. 67), our equine partner usually responds in kind.

For most professional polo players (I would venture this is also true for other equine sports) the horses become our obsession—finding the next champion, maintaining what we have, or perhaps worrying about the level of horsepower we are about to face in an

★ Flying High

One winter I was down in Florida announcing the 2022 Gauntlet of Polo® for ESPN. In the second and third legs of this event, one 10-goal player, Facundo Pieres, was flying high. He had found a way to turn around a so-so start to the season and now looked like he was under no pressure and expecting good things to happen. And his horses—an excellent string to begin with—seemed to have risen to a new level.

My cousin, Doo Little, a former professional polo player, commented: "I think his attitude translates to his horses."

The more I considered it, the more I agreed. Facundo went on to win the US Open and one of his mares, Mega Espia, was also named Best Playing Pony in the finals. We can't always feel like we're flying high, but as riders it should at least be our objective to put ourselves in a relaxed, positive frame of mind. And this attitude translates to our equestrian partners. //

upcoming match. But I, for one, could go overboard.

Working with Ani taught me that there is a time and place for taking care of the details of barns and horses but that, once those things are in order, it is time to let go.

By trusting ourselves and our partners we are calmer, and therefore better riders.

On entering almost any competitive venue, confidence—or lack thereof—in our ability to execute the task at hand is unconsciously conveyed to our equestrian partner. Like Bob Loomis wrote in his comprehensive work *Reining: The Art of Performance in Horses* (Equimedia, 1991): "If you think your horse can or can't, you are correct." So, if anything, through my sports psychology work, I worried less about the horses I was playing. And I trusted them more.

My Dream

Perhaps the line of questioning that most inspired me was something Ani called the four *resonance questions*, developed by the sports psychologist Doug Newburg:

/ **1** / "What feelings do you seek to experience in your sport?"

/ **2** / "What prepares you to experience these feelings?"

/ **3** / "What prevents these feelings from occurring?"

/ **4** / "How can you get these feelings back when they are lost?"

Sorting through my answers to these questions, I was eventually able to articulate my "dream" in my sport. Although I wrote the following passage when I was 10 goals and 39 years old, most of it still holds true for me today:

*The fall season has come and gone—some good, some bad. The other day I found a quote in a book—*Close Range *by Annie Proulx—which I had underlined years ago. It inspired me. Here is what it said about the "rough, bruising life" of a young rodeo rider: "...when he got on there was the dark lightning in his gut, a feeling of* ***blazing real existence****."*

This rings true for me. The dream for my polo is that feeling of ***blazing real existence****. It makes me feel alive. One way that it blazes is that my senses are wide open when playing, totally perceptive, and acutely sensitive. Maybe it's adrenaline, maybe it's the sense of challenge about using my skills toward a contest. Perhaps it's my "love-hate" relationship toward competitive situations—"Who is better?" Whatever, why-ever, I know that my gut blazes and I get that feeling of aliveness.*

My dream is to find this feeling of intensity and sensory connection when I am playing my game. I can even learn to appreciate it (enjoy it?) while it's there, and not only after the event. I reach this state through giving it my all; through thinking good thoughts, which enhance my confidence and ability to play well. Perhaps the stars just lined up correctly? This is the challenge: getting myself to this state of being. And it is another state

/ **8.2** / Amy showcasing her agility over the Santa Barbara Polo Club boards. She was a mare I felt at one with on the field.

of being—one of total awareness. I'm acting by "letting go" and letting my body lead. I'm not looking much at other players (teammates, opponents) or umpires. I'm trusting the strength of my horses; they feel a part of me. I may have a short outburst at an ump or opponent, but my anger quickly dissolves because there is no time. I have the next play to execute or prepare for. I am in it. My mind is comfortably locked on my objectives. These are simple and clear.

I am human and unnecessary thoughts do arise, even during best-best performances: "Geez, I'm playing one of my best games ever!" "I missed those two goals, I really want to finish my next chance—who's watching?" "I hope we win this one, I just got out-dueled." These thoughts are there, but when I'm living my dream and playing from my gut, I can deal with them. I recognize that it's okay to have them—everybody does—and bring myself back to my breath, my tree, or my "next play" mantra. Sometimes, when the feeling doesn't come easily in a particular match, the best technique is to try to "just be there," with a calm mind, and trust that the game will get into me. That can be enough. It allows the sport to bring out my instincts, my anticipation, and hopefully my total connection with my horses and what I am doing. Outside the parameters of my field, good things come—accolades, money, team offers—because of my connection inside that field, and because of my mindset, which ironically has a lot to do with not caring what people think outside the boards. Even my goals of playing at the highest level of the sport for a long time, of being a great 10-goal player, of fulfilling my potential, are really things outside the boards. What is inside is that emotion of ***blazing real existence****. Visit this often, go for it, and if it's meant to be, my goals will take care of themselves.*

My dream is to immerse in the feelings of intensity that I get from playing the game. I put myself in the most competitive situations possible because these challenges bring the "lightning in my gut." Love-hate it may be, but these big feelings are my dream. They exist because I care. (AS, 2003 "My Dream" Homework)

Freedom Comes Through Discipline

I believe competition is a time to emphasize our strengths, to focus on positive things in our control, to *trust* and *play*. This is the best way I've found for putting expectations to the side, *letting go*, and enjoying the performance. Famous dance choreographer Alvin Ailey said that "freedom comes through discipline." The discipline to prepare *to the teeth*, gives us the freedom to perform *all out*, thought-free.

I have come to believe that our mood, too, is in our control. "Being positive simply means that you see the choices in front of you," Ani says. We may sense that we woke up on the wrong side of the bed, or that our warm-up was a disaster, but it is usually possible to find (or invent) a positive lining—"bad rehearsal means good performance"—and shift focus onto the little things within our control. "What do I love about my sport?" is a question I ask myself before entering the competitive arena. For me: I love the ball, the teamwork, and the feel of the horse under me.

★ Competitor and Caretaker

When Pat Parelli stayed with us a few years ago for a week while he was competing his Quarter Horse youngsters in the Augusta Futurity, he figured out our training program pretty quick. A day or two into his stay, Pat said, "So I get it. You, Shelley, are the generalist, teaching the young horses, and Adam, you are the specialist, honing their skills when they're older." One veterinarian friend described it in different terms: Shelley was the "pitcrew chief" while I was the "NASCAR driver." //

First identify, and then focus on these aspects. Free yourself of result-oriented thoughts, and bring your awareness into the present. Feel your calming breath flowing in and out, see the texture of the footing, hear the cadence of your horse's stride. With your senses wide awake, and in the here and now, execute the task at hand to the best of your ability. Trust yourself. Trust your horse. Put your focus on the *doing*. After all, as Chungliang Al Huang and Jerry Lynch say in *Thinking Body, Dancing Mind,* "Focusing on the moment-by-moment joy and elation of the event will usually be reflected in winning outcomes." Win-win.

// Winning Point

The sports psychology principles I've shared in this chapter directly enhanced my partnerships with my horses. As riders, we understand how sensitive our mounts can be to the mood we transmit. Just settling into the saddle with a calm, balanced, and present state of mind is a giant step toward facilitating a great ride. When it came to game time, I still felt the "butterflies" (as did my horses), but I learned to view those sensations in a more positive light—I was *fortunate* to experience them. And riding my horses, trusting them, was the way I became immersed in the joy of competition. //

end *of* chapter 8

CHAPTER

9

Reflections on Competing

Grit and grace.

// Reflections on Competing

The Horse as a Competitive Partner

When it comes to the question of whether horses "enjoy" a sport, it is hard to say. But let's face it, your horse doesn't wake up in the morning and think, *Oooh, I can't wait to jump that course perfectly or execute a flying change or win a polo play.* He thinks, *Where's my food?* But, especially in horses that are bred to perform a certain job, I believe that they are undeniably better off when they are doing what they have been bred to do. Maybe it is just because I like to work, and I am anthropomorphizing. But let's admit that one of life's greatest hacks is exercise. For the mammalian brain, outdoor exercise checks all the boxes for building a healthy mind and body—true in the horse as much as in the human (see Gretchen Reynold's *The New York Times* article from May 12, 2021, entitled "How Exercise May Help Us Flourish"). The body's own feel-good hormones (*endogenous endocannabinoids* and *beta-endorphins* and *enkephalins*) increase their circulation and produce a cascade of positive effects, including lowering stress levels.

CHAPTER

9

/ 9.1 / Many horses do show eagerness to do their "job," whether it's on a playing field, out on the range, or like Chester is for me here on a cross-country course.

So, you're not going to convince me that *not* exercising a horse is doing it any favors.

But how do we know when to push and when to rest? Which factors come into the decision of whether or not to play/show/compete when the stakes are high? How do we conscientiously compete? I believe we have to understand deep in our hearts that we have prepared everything we are capable of preparing, and then and only then will we feel confident that we are entitled to make demands upon our horses. We must start with a horse suited to the job at hand, trained appropriately (confident that he is only going to be asked to do things he is capable of), and given every chance to be at his physical best. We also must ensure we are primarily using long-term thinking for the horse's welfare versus short-term gain.

These ideas sound straightforward, but it is of course very complicated to

★ What Does Your Horse Want to Hear?

What do you say to your horse when you get onto the field or head out of the start box or enter the ring? Do you say, "Trust me on this one," or "I will keep you safe today," or "Let's go, Tiger!" It makes a difference, depending on the horse. **//**

★ It's Never Make or Break

On making that call on whether to compete a horse or not: have confidence in yourself as an athlete, horseperson, and human that not competing this one horse on this one day won't make or break your career. There will be more opportunities in the future—maybe even better ones. //

achieve all of them (which is why we are writing a book about how to do it!).

Any doubt that surfaces can put a rider off-track. I often hear concerns from clients who witness veterinary procedures on their horses, or reach a deeper level of understanding about a soundness issue of their horses, and from that time forward have difficulty putting their horses back to full work. When questions lurk in the back of your mind about your preparation—"Did I cut short too many trot sets?" or "Did I jump high enough that last lesson?" or "Does the new feed give him enough energy?"—it can have a devastating impact on your confidence. Everything has to feel right before the competition begins.

At the professional, upper levels of any equine sport, I believe we as horsepeople have to acknowledge that everything can't be pretty all the time. Unless we abolish horse sport altogether, we have to make peace with the fact that finding the perfect line between not pushing hard enough and over-pushing is not always possible without trial and error. No person who has ever been a competitive athlete themselves would disagree. You don't achieve greatness without the proverbial blood, sweat, and tears. Our horses need to train hard also. Doing it well is the key.

No discussion of winning is complete without considering the horse's desire to win. Many books are written on sports psychology for the human athlete, but equestrians have to manage the psychology of the horse as well as their own! I find it fascinating to ponder how it varies among horses, and why. Is it different for mares, geldings, or stallions? Is it innate, so we can breed for it, or is it created, and thus we must train for it?

On gender: racehorse trainers certainly feel young colts are the most highly competitive; the vast majority of the top professional polo players prefer mares (about 95 percent of the top horses in polo are mares) for their drive and spirit. And male horses are traditionally castrated to enhance their tractability, which would seem to put geldings at a disadvantage in any equine sport where horses are in direct competition with each other. But when it comes to a horse being in the ring on his own and really trying to do his best, perhaps it simply comes down to character—which can be both bred and trained. And once you've got it, treasure it and handle it with kid gloves.

When Should Competition Be Over?

Regarding retirement (and I speak more to this issue in chapter 11—p. 157), I have heard many stories from clients who tell me about their geriatric horses doing so much better when they continue to "work." Recently I was texted a photo of a 20-year-old-plus patient, jumping a good-sized fence, perhaps 3'6", with the caption "Nick couldn't be happier that he is back doing his favorite thing." (The owner hadn't ridden him for a few years while she was busy training some younger horses.) Adam swears that one of our "retired" mares, Rio, grows a few inches and loses several years in attitude when she gets out on the polo field to "stick and ball" every now and then. Data does show that most humans do better with an active or even nonexistent "retirement." Of course, with horses, it is a little more complicated than with people, to know the right way forward.

It certainly depends on the situation, but perhaps the core issue is stress level. Would it be stressful for a horse who has competed at a high level for years to get turned out in a big field and not receive much human interaction after a lifetime of stalls and trailers and grooming? Maybe he would find it less stressful to be in light work, getting hacked and sticking to a familiar routine. Another horse, maybe particularly one who has been adjusted to turnout even during his prime, may know perfectly how to relax the minute his unshod feet hit green.

I received good advice from a child psychiatrist years ago when asking about making a school decision for my child. It was, in a nutshell, "If you listen, they will tell you." I believe the same is true for horses (although "listening" requires much more expansive perception in a horse than a child!). Older polo ponies will tell you because they don't want to enter the "throw-in" (when play is started by throwing it down the line-up of players and horses) or they tremble at the trailer. Jumpers will refuse fences or become grumpy in the barn. After appropriate trouble-shooting (ruling out medical and training issues) a solution can usually be found. Giving the horse to a younger rider often does the trick—horses quickly sense the drop in pressure and become the perfect schoolmaster. This is the winning

★ Be a Buddhist Olympian

There is a conflict between performance and practice. Riders have to figure out how to set goals and strive and be motivated, day after day, while simultaneously maintaining the calm, accepting persona of not grasping and allowing the slow natural evolution of training to take place. Since most equestrians ride their own horses every day, they must constantly seek harmony between these two. It's analogous to being a Buddhist on the face of things but underneath harboring a hidden Olympian. Striking the balance between "quiet" and "drive" is key for all athletes (and performers and strivers of any kind), but for equestrians, it is especially fraught as our energy is so transmissible to the creatures we are in partnership with. //

way—listen to your horse, pay attention to his behaviors, and the correct decision will present itself.

The Rider Part of the Equation

On a personal note, it is challenging to compete as an amateur rider while being a professional horseperson. You may know a lot but you can't always execute! I went through a phase with my current event horse where I thought he was so perfect I refused to ride with spurs or a whip. I wanted everything to be completely harmonious and him to be a truly willing partner. Or else, I idealistically believed, we wouldn't do it. Call it purism, I suppose. Then he "opted" not to jump one jump on a cross-country course. And I had to reconsider.

I've been called a "polite rider" more times than I can remember. I've even received the back-handed compliment, "If I believed in reincarnation I'd want to come back as your horse." Although flattering in one sense, coming from a high-powered coach it certainly meant my demands were decidedly on the lighter side! Recently I was cleaning out some drawers and perused some old dressage tests. In the collective marks I seemed to score consistently in the "8s" for gaits (and this was on my not-fancy Thoroughbreds) but "6s" for submission. I do prefer, and even often demand, obedience from my dogs

/ 9.1 / My favorite definition of dressage: *a combination of physical therapy and obedience, facilitated by nonverbal communication.*

and children, but my horse, well, he apparently often gets a hall pass!

I think I have these predispositions because I know enough to know that I don't want to overface my horse, but I also know enough to know that I may not have enough experience to decide where that line is. Especially when it comes to competing myself. Competing is a skill in and of itself, for both horse and rider. As with everything, practicing well is crucial to a successful outcome. Improving competitive skills takes time and experience and coaching. I remember visiting a top-tier gymnastics facility and written in huge letters on the back wall of the building was "Great gymnastics is not a result of a thousand repetitions. It is the result of a thousand corrections." I can't say it better myself.

In polo, I really only enjoy the lower-contact form of the game found in practices, with my sweet spot being training chukkers for young horses. Besides the obvious disadvantage I have of being a southpaw in a mandatory right-handed sport, I also have difficulty bringing myself to push a polo pony into the throw-ins, scrums, and bumps required in competitive games (maybe I know I'll be the one that has to take care of the horse back at the barn if he gets hurt!). Adam sometimes calls that aspect of the game

"trench warfare." But galloping around helping my mount learn how to follow the ball is all fun. It is truly play, not work.

For amateurs, it is difficult knowing a professional can do a better job keeping a horse's confidence up, and in those equestrian sports with higher levels of danger, keeping a horse safer. Some riders give up on the challenge for this very reason. It is particularly problematic when your horses live with you and you tend to all their daily needs—they evolve more into a pet than a competition partner. But it can be helpful to think honestly about your goals and focus on competence and improvement rather than results. In these instances, focusing on building a relationship and competing for fun can be your version of winning.

When I do compete, I like to be prepared. I do have my own sports psychology routine, gathered from various sources over the years. First of all, in training at home, I try to be disciplined about focusing on one thing every day that needs to be improved. I try to break down my goals into small, manageable ones. I do my best to not let negativity dominate my self-talk (easier said than done). I practice meditation and yoga to try and keep myself calm throughout my daily life, but I also rely on them (through breathwork and mindfulness) when it's crunch time. On competition day, I practice visualization, usually in my trailer immediately before going into the ring. (A pet peeve: someone saying dismissively, "Oh, that's all in your head." *In your head* is where it all happens.)

I have some games I play in my head with my horse when I am competing. For

★ Find a "Win" for You

If you are a person who is more focused on the welfare of the horse rather than on your own aspirations, you can still find a "win" in it for you. Get yourself an inspiring coach and surround yourself with supportive friends and family. What you do with your horse doesn't have to be in the form of traditional competition—undoubtedly, we all thrive with challenge, but there are different kinds of challenges worth pursuing. //

example, on a cross-country course when I am weaving around looking for the next obstacle, I'll try to think like a little kid on her pony: *Oooh...look! There's the jump! Let's go jump it!* (When I am thinking this, I *know* I am having fun!) Or when I am riding a dressage test and we have to do a turn-on-the-haunches I say to my horses: *Oops, sorry, I changed my mind. Let's go the other way.* Then when you come to the second turn on the haunches you *really* have to apologize and play along, because what can the horse possibly be thinking in that movement? *Geez, this idiot doesn't even know where she wants to go.* There is not a much worse fate for me than my horse thinking I'm an idiot!

Whenever I throw a leg over a horse and tell him where to go, I feel a responsibility to keep him safe. Whether that is stepping over a fallen wire on the ground or navigating holes or pointing him at a fence to jump, it is the same. It is truly amazing horses allow us to control them, and it is an honor I do not take lightly.

// Winning Point

Understanding what each participant—the horse and the rider—brings to the table on competition day is crucial to performance. Do you need a thermos of coffee for energy or do you need to develop a meditation practice to calm your mind? Does your horse need a relaxing acupressure session at the trailer or a little wakeup session on the rope upon arrival at the venue? When you do go out on the course or the field or into the arena, remember that you're benefitting from the bonds you've established with your horse through practicing all the many different mediums we've been discussing. It is time to enjoy.

end *of* chapter 9

CHAPTER

10

The Equine Athlete

Finding flow on your horse.

// The Equine Athlete

Having Skin in the Game

Is it a competitive advantage, or disadvantage, to play or show one's own horses? I have played many games with my own string and many with others' ponies, and the answer is nuanced.

For the first five years of my professional career, I never played a horse I owned, because I didn't own any. The pro-am model in polo back then—late 1980s and into the 1990s—involved the sponsors of high-goal teams fully mounting their professionals. For five consecutive summers, I played on a team based out of Cowdray Park in West Sussex, an hour's train ride south of London. The team patron owned approximately 35 horses, which he used to mount himself and three professionals each season for the Prince of Wales, Queens Cup, and Gold Cup tournaments.

I played essentially the same group of horses—Jimbo, Riojana, Revoltosa, Diana, Porcelana, Portenita, Jessica, Cola Corta—and I knew them intimately. During the off-season I tried lots of horses with the objective of

CHAPTER 10

/ 10.1 / Kanji (in the foreground) slamming on the "air brakes" the moment I thought about it. Look at her hind legs!

upgrading my string with one to two new ones for the following summer. I worked closely with an excellent Argentine groom, Fermine. I coordinated off-season turnout, transport (when new horses were being flown in from Miami or Buenos Aires), vet calls, farrier appointments, and the feed. In sum, I treated this group like my own string of horses. But the funds to pay for these ponies and their maintenance were not coming from my pocket. And, though I cared deeply for these horses, honestly, I had fewer worries about the longevity of their careers. I don't think I took shortcuts or unnecessary risks; however, winning in the short-term was very much a priority. This meant, for example, that I wouldn't hesitate to "double" (play two chukkers on) a favorite horse.

I personally experienced this "freedom" from ownership again, with one individual horse, even after I had begun owning and playing my own ponies. In 1996, I wanted to buy a chunky, bay mare named Kanji. The owners—who had bred, raised, and trained the Thoroughbred on their farm near Atlanta, Georgia—wanted to see me compete the mare in high-goal polo, but they didn't want to sell her. We eventually agreed on an annual lease of $5,000, for as long as I wanted to continue playing her. At the time, Kanji was 10, and I leased her for six

3
Temple
3
JEDI
POLO TEA
3

consecutive years. In a competitive sense, I think it was one of the best $30,000 expenditures I ever made. First, because she was an incredible pony: One game in Saratoga, New York, I scored five goals from her in the first chukker. It was the most goals I'd ever scored, all from the field, in a single chukker. And when I took her to England in 1999, she more than held her own against Australian media tycoon Kerry Packer's Ellerston ponies, then considered the best string in the world. And, second, because I played her free of worry, often doubling her in big games. And she stayed sound.

When I eventually stopped leasing Kanji, she was at an age (16) when most of my best horses gradually moved toward retirement, or at least a lower level of polo. In Kanji's case, she started getting sticky about "releasing," not jumping out of the throw-ins. Maybe she got wise to all the chaos that could ensue once she did explode and preferred to stay where she was. It was a subtle change, but enough to indicate that it was time to transition away from high-goal polo, which she did. We returned her to her owners round, sound, and happy. The owners' daughter played her indoors for several more years and then Kanji retired on the farm where she'd been born, and she foaled two bay fillies.

So, in this sense I believe a polo player is able to play "freer," with fewer worries, on a horse he does not own. I wonder if this is the same for riders in other horse sports. Everything else being equal, are professional eventers more confident on their own horses or on clients'? Most top jumpers and dressage horses are not "owned"

★ All in the Family

When I played on the same team with my brother, Andrew, I felt that our combined worth to the team was greater than the sum of our handicaps. Of course it would be! We knew each other like the back of our hands. We had trained together from the early days. And we fed off each other's strengths. When it comes to an equestrian teammate, it's the same dynamic. //

Your Ticket ★

In many sports, kids who have nothing to lose often grow up to be stars because they know success is their only ticket out of whatever difficult situation they were born into. There is some ineffable advantage to having skin in the game. And in equestrian sports, owning your own horses, and thus being responsible for them as partners as well as financially on the hook for their well-being, is perhaps the closest approximation. This is true regardless of the discipline in which you compete. //

by their riders, although the partnership that develops between horse and rider at that level can be likened to that between a caring "owner" and a horse. How would racetrack jockeys feel if they sometimes raced their own horses? In the sense of competition, it is an intriguing question.

At the height of my career, I was riding my own horses, and I was mounted to the teeth. And not because I spent more money than other players. Certainly, there was some element of luck. But mostly I think the reason is that *we*, meaning the team I was working with on these horses—Bento, Bete, and Shelley—used our combined skill and expertise to help those horses play well and stay healthy.

Bento and Bete worked as head grooms for 16 consecutive years for us, during the height of my career. They were expert caretakers of our horses, followed Shelley's veterinary suggestions to the letter, and took as much pride as any of us in the successes of the amazing animals they cared for. The continuity of their conscientious care—knowing our horses as individuals for many years—brought its own advantages.

Fortunately, horses usually improved (or, at least, looked good) under me, and this is why many people were willing to sell their horses to us (or lend them, as was the case with Kanji). They wanted Shelley to be making the animal welfare decisions, and me to be playing them (and, hopefully, winning BPP prizes on them).

And when I got to work with a horse on our own farm in Aiken—play him in a medium goal season, practice him in "3v3s" on our small field surrounded

★ Notches on the Stick

A player's decision about "doubling" a horse—playing him two chukkers in a match—is a complicated one. If, like one friend, Sugar Erskine (a teammate for the 2004 Argentine Open), you believe a pony has an allotted number of full-on, seven-minute chukkers in his career's "gas tank," then you want to be very smart about if and when you choose to double. In other words, if every hard chukker puts another notch on that stick, then the ones that are doubled frequently are likely to have shorter careers.

Shelley and I would argue that picking the right points to rest a horse can grow the overall length of a horse's career (the length of the stick); but Sugar's point is well-taken, and relevant to a player's decision about whether to play horses twice in a single game for all, or most, of those finite number of chukkers. The other issue is that if you play your favorite horse two chukkers in every match, the risk of injury goes up exponentially—you can almost assume that you are halving (or greater) the longevity of that horse's competitive career.

Today, many top players have a preference for playing horses half-chukkers, or even less, and then bringing them back, sometimes more than once, for a few more minutes at critical points in the game. The advantages of this are less risk of injury and never being caught on a tired horse. The disadvantages are that many of these changes must be made on the fly—like switching lines in ice hockey—which can leave your teammates with three versus four for a spell, and, at least for me, it upsets my flow if I enter a chukker already thinking that I need to change a few minutes in. Plus, you are assuming your spare is as good as the one you're on! It's hard for me to want to get off a good, fit horse that has only played three minutes.

There are similar questions in other equestrian sports. Jumpers "only have so many jumps in them" and reiners only so many slides. Remembering the notches on the stick, and the length of the stick, is important. //

by a fence, work with him at liberty in the round pen—it was like adding layers to our partnership of confidence and trust in each other, so that by the time we travelled together to a high-goal season in Florida, Santa Barbara, the United Kingdom, Argentina, or New England, we had been through some stuff, some steps, together. We were ready! Hopefully, necessarily, we could trust each other in a pinch on the field. So if I was riding Pumbaa (who I bought as a five-year-old), Hale Bopp (at six), Bag Lady (age four), there was an attitude of confidence, bordering on arrogance, that came both through their training foundation and having Shelley determine the ideal care for these individuals year-round. We had trained, we had put in the work together, and if another combo was going to touch us on the playing field, they better have something special.

Now age 58, I may be deluding myself, but I still feel this way on my best horse.

If you can only be as good as your horse, there's one more factor that plays into competing better on your own horses: You are *all in*...with no excuses. It's a different level of commitment. At least it was for me. And, even though it involved a huge risk, as well as a leap of faith about being able to "make this work," taking this step was fundamental toward my becoming the best player I could be. I may have had a few more worries off the field, but I was more confident on it.

> ”
>
> The fastest way to accomplish a lot is to go slowly.
>
> Bob Loomis

Going Fast Slowly

When I give polo lessons, I encourage students to *swing slow and easy*, and try to *let the mallet head do the work*. When we increase the speed of the horse, the objective is to retain the same fluid swing, and start it sooner. The goal is to go for timing and not force. Easier said than done, but this is the objective.

The same is true when you jump up into higher-goal polo. Often people's first thought is, "It's faster polo, so I need to *run* faster," but nothing could be

/ 10.2 / Pumbaa how I like them: attentive, relaxed, coiled. Exemplifying *easy power.*

further from the truth. In order to arrive at the ball with some time and space, we need to *think* faster, plan sooner, but not *go* faster. Making haste with a quiet mind is the idea, or in a manner of speaking—*make haste slowly.* As my teammate Alfonso Pieres told me once in an effort to stop me from running and get me thinking more: "It's not a horserace out there."

I always gravitated toward the best polo I could play, because I realized that playing *faster* polo would make me quicker mentally. Then, when you bring the level down a notch—say from the Argentine Open to Florida pro/am polo—because the speed of play is slower, you find yourself with time and space. And it's a great feeling. But it's not always possible to travel to Argentina, or even play at a higher level, in order to get sharp. So I developed other strategies as well. Imagery was something I used nearly every day—imagining scoring goals, or visualizing plays that gave me difficulty and finding ways to get through them smoothly. And then I came up with the idea that, in practice, if I went no faster than everyone else (sometimes even a bit slower), I would be forced to use my anticipation to win plays. So I tried to win plays with my head, and not my horse. When it came to game time, and we were all going wide open, hopefully I'd still be arriving first to the plays because of my anticipation. With mental sharpness, and riding a good horse, you never feel like you're in a rush; in fact, at times it feels like the game slows down for me. Some athletes describe this sensation like going in slow-motion, but quickly (if that makes any sense). In other words, you need to *think fast in order to go slow.*

Olympic swimmer Jeff Rousse—three-time gold medalist and former

The Watercourse Way ★

How does my horsemanship and riding benefit the horse? I try to ride like water. I want to make moderations of speed and gait gradual, or at least smooth, like shifting through the gears of a car. I like the feeling of a horse melting into the ground on a stop. But I've always known that checking and turning takes less out of a horse than stopping to zero and then having to restart. And on my most balanced horses, I want my flying changes to be so subtle that an observer can't see any movement of my body. I always imagine my lower body quiet, rooted to the ground through the horse, and my upper body lifted toward the heavens, light and free, turning my head like an owl to see all around. My attitude on the field is to be like the river flowing around boulders, finding the path of least resistance. This sounds silly when I write it, but it is what I do.

I have always admired the skilled riders and horses that look as if they are flowing on the field or course, whatever sport it may be. "Memo" Gracida and Miguel Novillo Astrada (both former teammates) are two 10-goalers I liked to watch play for this quality. They never looked like they were in a rush; in fact, sometimes they appeared to be going in slow motion, but they were still arriving at the ball first! If I were a horse, I'd want to win plays like this—with anticipation and flow. And I think their ponies, and hopefully mine too, "go better" because we ride with this attitude.

The thing is that once a horse knows his job, whatever that job may be, it's about keeping yourself in balance and staying out of his way. It's like that cutting horse who's zeroed in on his steer. At least from outside the arena, it looks like all the rider needs to do is stay quiet over the horse's withers and let his instincts prevail. //

world-record holder in three separate events in the 1990s—named a similar phenomenon. "Easy speed" was what he called the ability to go 100 percent of your maximum speed, while exerting only 80 percent effort. Rousse described the way he got into the zone: "Utilize your years of training, take confidence from all the work you're doing now, then relax a little bit during competition, and try to use only 80 percent effort." In other words, *try easier*.

Argentine polo great Nachi Heguy said the trick is to "play fast, but never hurry." I would venture that the same is true for most equestrian sports. Observing Olympic event riders on the cross-country course in Japan in 2020 illustrated this concept. I love to watch the horse and rider combos that can gallop a stretch toward a single obstacle, and then take that jump flat, with no apparent change in stride. I know this skill helps to "make time," or at least be closer to the ideal time, but there's a lot of communication going on pre-jump that helps the pair appear so fluid and effortless. These pairings are *in tune* with one another, *on the same page*, practiced, and smooth. And in the case of combination fences—particularly in and out of water—there's so much happening between those two obstacles that, to me, it looks like pure chaos: there's the landing into the water; the rider grabbing for wet reins while wriggling to regain her seat; the horse either waiting for direction or guessing at one; the rider guiding with uneven reins and one foot searching for that stirrup; the pair finally pointed at the next obstacle,

★ Don't Be a Distraction

It is important to remember that in equestrian sport we (the rider) are not just doing this slowing-down and calming practice for ourselves—it is also for the horse. Both our physical and mental tension is transferred to the horse through our contact via the saddle and the reins. Different horses will respond in different ways, but even if they can "handle" this pressure, it is certainly not helpful. They need to focus on their job without the distraction of a tense rider. //

and they're only two strides out, but it's kicking uphill now, and there's only one way to go.... Now *this* is where all that training comes in. *Hang on!*

I've never evented, but I'd be willing to bet that it's trust and instinct that these pairs rely on between jumps, and that—even in this moment of apparent mayhem—calm minds prevail. As Chinese philosophy understands, "it is of great importance to achieve an inner peace which will allow you to act in harmony with the times" (I Ching 52).

During my own competitions I feel like, if I can remain calm, I almost can't make mistakes. And usually it is my breathing that aids in this attempt (not always successful) to maintain calm. Even in the turmoil of a polo game or a cross-country course or a timed jump-off, I believe a quiet mind is critical to this ability of *going fast, slowly*.

// Winning Point

In the prologue to his and Jerry Lynch's *Thinking Body, Dancing Mind* (Bantam Books, 1994) Chungliang Al Huang writes: *Tao is the purest simplicity of being in accordance with nature—the watercourse way.* The water running in a river is soft yet strong. It yields to rocks and flows through the channels. Similar to the "easy power" I referenced in chapter 8 (p. 115), "trying easier" was a concept that helped me relax on my horse. Rather than tensing and thereby causing an equal and opposite reaction from my equine partner, I could try to "go with the flow." And this is probably why it helps me to imagine riding a horse like water. Eyes where you want to go. Now sit back and enjoy the ride. //

end *of* chapter 10

CHAPTER

11

Horse Essentials

Follow facts not fads.

// Horse Essentials

Let Horses Be Horses

Horse stewardship is usually best served by keeping things as natural as possible. This doesn't imply that scientific research is useless, but rather, that there is an art to finding the balance between experimentation and what thousands of years of evolution has wrought upon the horse when we consider optimizing his care. This is nowhere truer than in housing horses—would that every horse was so lucky to live on a farm with extensive pasture! There are just so many reasons: physically, horses evolved to travel a minimum of five miles per day; grazing serves as the best postural rehabilitation available; mental benefits abound, especially if they are turned-out with other horses for socialization. One of my favorite things to watch is a horse cavorting away after being released into a large pasture he knows signifies "R&R."

The vast majority of horses in the United States are companion animals or lower-level competition horses who will thrive in a natural environment.

CHAPTER

”

My favorite social media clips from the Olympics? The ones from when the equine stars had returned home and were let loose in their paddocks and pastures, free to buck and run and roll.

If they live outside in a grassy field with shelter and a friend or two, are barefoot, and don't have to travel by trailer too much, owners will be surprised at how little human intervention is necessary to maintain their health. When I guest lecture for the US Polo Association, I will often half-joke that if all polo ponies lived on pasture and did all their conditioning in sets most veterinarians would be out of a job!

An entire movement has sprung up around this theory—if you haven't heard of it, it is called *Equitation Science*. It is dedicated to improving horse welfare and health via science-based techniques. It is a little ironic to use scientific methods to prove that natural care works best, but regardless, if it helps horses, I'm all in.

★ Say No to Horse Jails

I have to admit that sometimes in my job I find myself working in a certain situation at a barn where my overwhelming feeling is of sadness for the horses in whatever program they are in. They are stuck in stalls, fed not very often and at the whim of humans, and have little or no equine companionship. I think to myself, *We must find a better way to do this.* Just say no to horse jails. //

★ It Was Always the Better Way

Here are some recent examples of the irony where scientific research "discovers" that natural methods are superior:

1. The FEI recently banning the clipping of horses' whiskers.
2. A 2016 study showing that horses fed a high-grain ration spend more time being alert for signs of danger than those on an all-hay diet.
3. A 2020 *The Horse* magazine article promoting not clipping legs in order to prevent the common skin condition "scratches."
4. Researchers recommending feeding horses in groups and multiple times a day.

(Look it up, if you're interested; there may be a specialist near you who can help make adjustments at your farm. And as an aside, I've always had the fantasy of fencing the periphery of our farm and just letting the horses run wild. Even though they are often living in pastures of 5 to 20 acres, how much fun would it be to see them free on a couple hundred?)

My theory on turnout (defined by weeks to months of living in a pasture with no human-enforced exercise) is that if you don't structure it on your timetable your horse will "pick" the most inopportune time (such as in the middle of a show or competition season) for an enforced rest. Every horse should have at least one, ideally two, scheduled rest-and-relaxation periods each year. If you are not lucky enough to be able to do it on your own farm, then finding an appropriate facility is paramount. A good turnout experience can be incredibly healthful for your horse if done well. It can also be a disaster if unsafe fencing, poor shelter, or inexperienced personnel put your horse's well-being at risk.

Consider your goals for turnout and put some money toward making the most of the time your horse gets to be on rest and relaxation. Common goals of turnout include: physiological rest; mental rest from the stresses of travel, competition, and temporary stabling; physical rehabilitation from clinical or subclinical injury; socialization training; and weight control (either gain, loss, or maintenance) measured by body condition score (or BCS—see p. 167). Deciding which of these five are relevant to your horse's situation should help you determine the type of turnout you need. The field size, the terrain of the pasture, the quality and type of grass, the length of time, which and how many other horses the horse will live with, and the amount of contact with humans are all factors to consider. Assess your horse's needs, find a turnout facility that meets them, and you will gain a healthy and happy horse in a few weeks or months who is primed to get back to work.

On Retirement

Retirement is a thorny issue in the equine industry. One thing I witness as

/ **11.1** / Horses turned out at New Haven Farm, experiencing "grazing therapy."

★ Barns for Us

All horse people love a barn. But admit it, we need barns for us, not for them. Barns ease human interactions with horses—they make it easier to shoe them, feed them grain, and ride them—all things which horses do not intrinsically need. //

a veterinarian in the United States is the disparity between the beginning of a horse's life and its end. Especially in the racehorse industry, it is apparent that very wealthy individuals are often breeding the mares and producing the foals, while often it is "backyard" owners who are rescuing horses from kill pens and providing horses with "forever" homes. But the numbers don't add up—the fact is, most horses do not end life in happy retirement. And it is unconscionable.

The breed registries are the first line of defense—they need to hold owners accountable for the foals they produce. It could be fairly straightforward: breeders need to guarantee they will provide retirement for the same number of horses that they register every year. Or guarantee (with microchipping this is easy) that every horse they foal can always come back to the farm. Sport registries are another governing body with clout, and that already have horse and owner information, and could take some positive steps to demand better accountability for the welfare of equine retirees.

Adam and I have struggled with this issue ourselves, as it is a huge financial commitment to feed and care for an older horse until natural death. Some of our horses have remained with us at New Haven Farm. We have found great retirement homes for others. We have found homes for horses that we then later found to be unsatisfactory and have had to retrieve them. And in a few heartbreaking cases we discovered a home was no longer suitable, but too late. We tragically sent one mare off who died under dubious circumstances when turned out in a large pasture. That particular mare was very valuable and had been sent for breeding purposes. My hope had been that because she was expensive, people would take better care of her. But this was not the case. We lost another mare to a medical mistake when she was being bred after her polo career was over. These are the ones I lose sleep over.

One of my financial goals of the last 10 years has been to not "have to" sell or give away any more of our horses. If the perfect home comes along, where both parties (horse and new owner) benefit, then great, but if not, every horse can live out their days with us. And that means that when the time comes we have to make a decision to euthanize them, which is extremely hard to do for an animal that has been a part of your life for so long. At least, with us, it can happen without stress, on the farm our horses know as home. We usually plant a tree over the grave.

Every person who buys a horse should feel some responsibility for what happens to that horse for the rest of his life. It is so sad when horses change hands so often, and end up so often in the wrong hands. It is no wonder that the term "horse trader" is such a pejorative in the English language.

Veterinarians will usually refuse to euthanize a healthy horse under a certain age just to relieve the owner of the responsibility of caring for the horse. It is a difficult policy—weighing the quality-of-life issue on one hand with the right to life on the other—but one which would be made much easier if other equine organizations "had our back," so to speak, on

★ The Gold Standard

Godolphin, the global Thoroughbred breeding operation and horseracing team founded by His Highness Sheikh Mohammed bin Rashid Al Maktoum, has recently made a commitment to taking care of all the horses they have ever bred until the end of their lives, if necessary. I hope this becomes the gold standard for the industry. //

the issue. My rule of thumb is that a horse under the age of 25 needs to have a serious medical problem to warrant euthanasia. But is it ethical to *not* euthanize a horse, knowing that it has a good chance of being abused or neglected? I don't know the answer to that one, as animal cruelty laws vary so much in how they are enforced.

There are many wonderful equine rescue centers dotted around the country. But most I've visited are funded by charity, operating on a shoestring budget, and staffed by workers earning minimum wage. Certainly some of the horses receiving care at these facilities were undoubtedly bred by billionaires. Where is the fairness in that?

You Are What You Eat

Feeding horses is unfortunately as subject to fads and misinformation as is feeding humans. My first question always is: would a wild or feral horse have eaten that 100 years ago? As we have already discussed, keeping it natural is where to start. Horses' gastrointestinal systems evolved over millennia to graze almost continually, so most time and money and effort of a horse owner ought to be spent on considering the source of forage. That may mean taking care of pastureland, cover-cropping, or it may mean investing in good hay. In virtually all situations, free choice is optimal. Many people

★ The Next Bite

We had a laid-back homebred named Souvenir. One day when he was three years old and I had just finished a couple of months' worth of training on him, I went to turn him out with another youngster, a mare who was relatively new to our farm, and in my estimation, had arrived a little skinny. It was early spring and the grass wasn't up yet, and I had laid hay piles out in the pasture for them. They were going to have a few months of "R&R." As I took the halters off, the mare rushed the hay and aggressively protected her pile. As Souvenir ambled over to the second pile, I could just hear him say, *Jeez, relax. It's not like there's ever not enough food around here.* Unlike her, he had spent his whole life not worried about where his next bite would come from! **//**

are concerned about a horse getting too fat, but I have yet to meet a horse who is fed well, exercised well, and obese. Just like in humans, scarcity (or perceived scarcity) can cause a concern about food availability. Most horses can find a natural homeostasis in their weight when offered free-choice food, *if* they are in proper work.

It bears repeating: grass and hay should provide the vast bulk of foodstuffs for all horses. For most horses, they can be almost the sole food. Grains are only necessary when the horse's caloric needs, usually due to moderate to high levels of exercise, can't be met by forage alone. It is therefore a given that the most attention and money should be spent on procuring the best forage possible. It is not an overstatement to say that what your horse eats affects all aspects of his health and personality, and will determine his ability to perform athletically on any given day. It is also a given that each horse will be different, and therefore individualizing nutrition for each horse in each situation is vital.

One exception to the "natural is best" mantra when it comes to feeding horses is the inclusion of fat in their diet. Scientific research really helped the horse community on this one: Studies conducted in preparation for the 1996 Olympics in Atlanta found that horses on a high-fat diet were less subject to heat stress. It turns out fat burns cooler in the horse's body than protein, which has big advantages for exercising in hot and humid conditions. And a beneficial side effect was found—horses were less spooky! They performed the classic umbrella test (walk

★ FFF

Adam had a teammate in the early nineties who was dealing with a very talented but high-strung mare. Eventually they switched to an all-hay diet, and voila, it worked. Blue Cabin won the Best Playing Pony prize when they won the 26-goal Gold Cup tournament in 1992.

Remember the mantra "FFF" (Feed Forage First), and you can't go too wrong. The benchmark forage recommendation is 2 to 3 percent of body weight; to take an easy example, a 1,000-pound horse would require about 20 to 30 pounds of hay daily.

(Recently I found another FFF I like even better than mine! I follow Brianna Noble @urbancowgirl510, and her FFF is Forage Freedom Friends. Amen.). //

★ Nutritional Triangle

My simple take on nutritional foodstuffs can be envisaged by a triangle.

1. The bottom and by far largest layer is fiber: grass, hay, beet pulp.

2. The next, considerably smaller layer is fat: rice bran, seeds such as flax or chia, omega-3 rich oils.

3. Last, in tiny amounts at the top is complex, natural carbohydrates: barley, oats, corn. Sugar really has no place in the equine diet.

a horse out of the barn and have someone pop open an umbrella) and the horses on a high-fat diet were significantly less reactive than those on a same-calorie but made-up-of-carbohydrate-and-protein diet. Ever since, I have assiduously recommended adding fat in the form of flax, hemp, or rice bran to the diet of any horse who needs more calories than forage alone can provide. Other health benefits include increased stamina, and decreased colic and laminitis risk.

Modern science has also discovered nutritional requirements for the ill or pregnant horse; food-allergy testing is another breakthrough. These innovations are extremely beneficial to many horses. I also utilize the ancient tradition of Chinese veterinary food therapy in my practice. It is based on the same principles as acupuncture and herbal medicine and assesses food by how it interacts energetically with bodily processes.

Body Condition Scoring

Body condition scoring (BCS) is a very useful tool to learn as it makes what can be very subjective ("That horse is too skinny") into a more objective description ("He's a BCS '3' so doesn't belong on the polo field"). With a little experience, not only can you develop an eye for assessing weight, and most importantly how that weight is distributed on the horse's body, but you can also apply it to learn what your own horse's ideal weight is. Depending on their job, and their particular character, most ridden horses come in at a "4," "5," or "6" for their ideal BCS. In our barn when we had a string of top polo ponies playing a competitive season, even though they were all required to do the same work, we learned that they each required a distinct weight to optimize their performance. We discovered what that weight was through trial and error.

★ Adam's Story of Regenerative Agriculture

One "natural" innovation we have tried on our farm recently is *cover cropping*. Its primary objective is to improve the health of our soil and consequently the lives of the horses who subsist on these pastures. In 2020 I was influenced by reading Gabe Brown's book *Dirt to Soil* (Chelsea Green, 2018), which touted the benefits of regenerative agriculture for profit as well as environmental sustainability. Three key principles stuck with me: *no-till planting, cover cropping*, and *diversity of plants* (as well as animals, when possible).

I found a local advisor, Reed Edwards, who had been successful with these practices on his own hay and horse farm in Laurens, South Carolina (70 miles to our north) and in the fall of 2021 I drilled a "cocktail" of cold weather cover crops on 30 acres of our pastures. Based on his own experience, Reed—who was extremely generous with his advice—helped devise our mix, which included: oats, brome, rye, hairy vetch, three types of clover, flax seed, chicory, and daikon radish. I rented the no-till seeder from the Aiken Soil & Water Conservation District office and set to work. It was my first time seeding anything larger than a garden box, and it took me three runs (over the same pasture) until I was finally dropping seed at an appropriate rate. I will never make those mistakes again! We rested these pastures for approximately six weeks after planting and then turned the horses back out on them with lots of new greenery sticking up through the yellowing warm weather grasses.

There is a natural symbiosis among these plants that helps raise the amount of organic matter in the soil, which is important because soil rich in organic matter has better retention of water and is therefore more drought-resistant. The legumes (clovers and vetch) draw nitrogen from the atmosphere and fix it to their roots; this effect of "harvesting sunlight," which happens even during cold weather months, negates the need for any additional commercial fertilizer. The deep-rooted plants like radish and chicory draw minerals from the subsoil. Some farmers say they can smell rich soil and that it has the consistency of chocolate cake (meanwhile, I'm still learning how to operate the seeder).

These are all great benefits but most importantly for us, these annual cover crops provided winter forage for our horses during the months when our bermuda and bahia grasses went dormant. Our horses looked happy out there nibbling on greenery! We also were able to feed less alfalfa (60 percent less is our best estimate), a savings which more than compensated for any additional expenditure for seed and drill rental. It felt like a win-win-win: for our horses, our land, and our bottom line.

(If you are interested in learning more about how to take care of our plants and animals in a sustainable manner, we recommend the following, along with *Dirt to Soil:* Doug Tallamy's *Nature's Best Hope* (Timber Press, 2020) and John Chester's documentary film *The Biggest Little Farm*.). **//**

★ BCS by the Numbers

Body condition scoring is graded on a scale of "2" to "9." Horses ideally should all fall in the "4" to "7" range.

BCS "4": Abdomen tucked up, ribs visible, good muscling. Ready to compete at the top level. Tomorrow.

BCS "5": Abdomen flat, ribs not visible but palpable, good muscling. Most horses can maintain this weight with proper nutrition and work fairly easily.

BCS "6": Abdomen flat, ribs not palpable, good muscling. Ideal weight for the beginning of a competitive season for endurance athletes and often the weight of choice for show ring hunters and other pleasure horses.

BCS "7": Round abdomen and fat deposits at tailhead, good muscling. Often the weight horses come in at after turnout.

Undesirable body condition scores: Low BCS horses (BCS "3" and below) show their bones, lose muscle, are underweight, and risk organ damage due to malnutrition. High BCS horses (BCS "8" and above) start to show fat deposits in multiple areas, don't have sufficient muscling for their mass, and are prone to medical problems associated with obesity.

When it comes to *supplementation*, I believe the jury is still out on whether it is a science or a scam. All too often I witness that supplement use is simply compensating for poor choices in how horses are housed and ridden (for example, not providing horses access to grass pasture, or failing to condition horses properly). We all need to ask first: how can I ride and house my horse better so fewer supplements are necessary?

Unfortunately, excess supplementation is also often a symptom of poor veterinary work since it can patch over inadequate diagnostic rigor. I certainly use them, but prefer well-researched brands, and demand that they be specific and targeted in both intended use and temporally. I have all too often had a new client who over the months or years has been told to add supplement after supplement until their feed room looks like a tack shop with countless jars and bottles. No one ever told them to *stop* anything. It takes some work to go through and assess what is really needed but is well worth the time and effort.

If I had to name two supplements I regularly feed or prescribe to others, they would be:

/ **1** / Omega-3s—Good anti-inflammatories, good fats; studies show that they increase stride length.

/ **2** / L-Lysine—An amino acid that helps with immune system regulation and can be the limiting factor in poor topline and poor hoof growth.

"

All equine athletes need to maintain enough muscle mass to power themselves, protect their joints, and have enough "gas in the tank."

Conditioning the Whole Horse

Proper conditioning is a very important factor in getting the most out of a competition horse. There are two elements to fitness—*cardiovascular* and *musculoskeletal*. They are equally important. Both are ideally developed through long slow distance work (LSD). Imagine a triangle of time spent riding your horse. Walking is at the bottom of the triangle, comprising the vast majority of minutes spent in the saddle, particularly when "legging-up" horses after periods of rest, but also during a competition season. An hour-long walk maintains muscle tone and suppleness without any risk whatsoever. Flatting and trot sets would take up the second-most amount of time.

★ Keep It Simple

In all areas of life, it pays to be cognizant of where and how we spend our time and money. It is true that many things to do with horses are very expensive. Try your best to not get sucked into needing too much unnecessary "stuff." Your horse actually has pretty simple tastes and requirements. //

★ Tips for Feeding the "Hot" Horse

1. Feed Forage First (FFF)

2. High fat

3. 1000 milligrams Thiamin (Vitamin B1) per day

4. 15 milligrams magnesium oxide per day

Sports-specific training comes in near the top, and performance is at the very tip.

Once attained, horses maintain their cardiovascular fitness very easily. This is one place it doesn't help to extrapolate from humans—we lose our cardiovascular fitness in a matter of hours (24 to 48). Horses takes days or even weeks to lose theirs. They have wonderful, large hearts. The better for riding them.

Maintaining musculoskeletal fitness is more of an issue for horses—especially sport horses who are asked to do somewhat "unnatural" things. It behooves us to remember that both bones and muscle are tissues that are adaptive—that is, they react to use and pressure. They need to be stressed to become stronger. The LSD work helps with injury prevention in these tissues, as they have time to adapt and change according to the work they are asked to do. It is also so important to remember that, just like humans, horses vary a lot in their physiological capabilities. Therefore, what is an appropriate amount of conditioning for one horse does not necessarily translate into what will be appropriate for his stablemate. Programs in conditioning need to be individualized.

One of the most important distinctions to learn as a rider is distinguishing the difference between a horse that is "heavy" (not quite fit), and a horse that is "spent" (tired). They can feel the same to the rider, but they are obviously treated in an opposite manner. Knowing the back story is important—nine times out of ten I can ask what the horse has done in the last two weeks and know the answer! I love it when my client speaks Spanish,

/ 11.2 A & B / Riding "sets"—exercising more than one horse at one time—on a farm is pure enjoyment for horses and riders, as well as a very efficient way to condition both.

because the Spanish words for these two syndromes—*pesado* and *pasado*—even sound alike. It makes parsing the difference more real. A few recent media interviews with top eventers have interestingly veered toward this topic, with unanimity on the opinion that *less is more* when it comes to working their top horses. For them, overwork is more of a problem than underwork. If you have horses in a fairly strenuous program, it really helps to keep track of their exercise, especially the number of "maximum effort days" (heavy training or competing). When it is written down, it is easier for the human brain to acknowledge and assess.

Consistency is crucially important for muscle health. Some programs go so far as to test muscle enzymes on a daily basis to

A

★ Recipe for Success

There are many foundational exercises that cross disciplines in the multifaceted world of equine sports. Cross-training can be so beneficial for mental breaks and physical strengthening. Eventers can do conditioning like fox hunters (long medium-speed rides) or polo ponies (20-minute trot sets); dressage horses can do cavalletti and gymnastics; polo ponies can work cattle; and all horses benefit from hacking on varied terrain in order to develop self-carriage. There are so many talented people in the horse world to learn from. Taking the best practices from different equestrian disciplines is a recipe for success. //

provide immediate feedback on how hard to push the next day. Short of this, a regular work schedule based on good training principles for your sport will go far to prevent tying up and other muscle injuries as well as optimize muscle building. A hard-and-fast rule with horses: no "weekend warriors"! Also, the easy way out is almost never the correct way. If you read an advertisement that says, "Use...for guaranteed increased performance" run the other way! It is almost never that simple!

Farriery

I completely subscribe to the old adage, "No foot, no horse." Don't skimp on this one—hire the very best farrier you can afford. Having said that, however, it is very economical to invest some time and money into learning from the "wild" horses of the world, and if you have an experienced practitioner you can trust, consider the possibility of properly trimming your horse to be comfortable barefoot. For soundness and longevity, providing your terrain allows it, barefoot can be best. It allows the natural shock-absorbing function of the foot to operate properly, reducing concussive forces and promoting healthy stresses to stimulate growth. In areas with good footing (and given the horse's conformation and hoof health allow it), the innovation of shoeing should only be necessary for upper-level sport horses. The minute you place a shoe on a horse's foot, you alter the biomechanics. Make sure whoever is doing it is experienced and competent. I can't stress enough that this is not a place to cut corners.

★ Tips for Feeding the "Flat" (Dull) Horse

1. Increase feed to attain a BCS of "5" (can increase one point by feeding 6 megacalories (Mcal) more per day for 60 days, which is the equivalent of 4 pounds of grain or 6 to 8 pounds of hay or 4 to 12 hours of grazing).

2. Fat supplementation (the best sources are high omega-3 seeds or oils such as flax, chia or hemp, or rice bran).

3. Check Vitamin E, Selenium, and Vitamin B12 levels.

4. If in hot or humid conditions, add electrolytes. To make your own, mix two to three parts NaCl (which is normal table salt) to one part KCl (which you can find in the grocery store as "lite salt"). //

★ Ask Permission

I try to remember every day to offer the bridle, saddle pad, and saddle to my horse to sniff before tacking him up. It seems only fair that before I strap something onto his body, I let him know what it is. "Asking permission" creates respect and reminds me how grateful I am that this large powerful being allows me such liberties. //

Sometimes innovative thoughts come from hard knocks, or as is said, *necessity is the mother of invention*. This was true in the summer of 2004 in Santa Barbara, California. One moment I was standing on the sidelines with one eye on the game while chatting with an old friend I hadn't seen in years; the next I was off like a shot, sprinting across what seemed a never-ending expanse of green. Tequila was down. Tequila was a brown Thoroughbred mare unequalled in Adam's string at laterality—she swooped in and out of traffic at full speed up and down the polo field like a fighter jet. But this turn had bested her—a slippery spot perhaps—and she was indeed lateral, this time flat out on her side on the ground.

By the time I arrived an older cowboy who had been close by was at her head trying to make her get up. She was motionless. I asked him to get on her head and keep it down with one knee on her neck. He lifted his eyes, took in this girl in a tee-shirt, shorts, and running shoes and kept doing what he was doing. This had happened to me before. I hated doing it, but I knew I had to pull rank.

"I'm a vet. Come around to this side and put a knee on her neck and keep her head down," I asked again, more firmly this time.

My educated guess after a quick assessment was that Tequila had simply had the wind knocked out of her and she needed that girth loosened—the faster the better. At this point the cowboy complied, and I was able to safely reach around

★ Adam's Take on Trying New Things

A few years ago, Shelley encouraged me to try playing my horses barefoot for local tournaments at home in Aiken, South Carolina. Even though it was common for me to ride and practice younger horses barefoot, shoeing for tournament play was just something that everybody did! But Aiken is blessed with sandy soil, a big reason it is a thriving, multi-disciplined horse community, and the more I considered it, the more psyched I got to give it a try.

Shelley explained that from a veterinary perspective, the small amount of additional slippage (of a bare hoof sliding a couple inches over grass) is not only natural, but serves to reduce the strain on the joints and soft tissue in the lower legs. Think: in youth sports like soccer and baseball, metal spikes are not permitted due to risk of injury to developing joints. An additional advantage is that, if your horses live together in pastures (like ours do), there is far less risk of a horse sustaining a serious injury from a kick. Even though we try to pasture the friends together and keep the odd fighter on his own, accidents do happen. And—sadly we know from experience—steel shoes can break bones.

We had a good barefoot trimmer, Marilyn Gilligan, who taught us the ropes. And Shelley and I both began trimming our own horses. So an additional advantage was that during the tournaments I would not have any shoes coming off with concomitant last-minute scrambles to find a farrier to reset them right before a game. If any moderations needed to be made, I could take care of them myself.

And so, I played two tournaments barefoot. In the tent, before my first game with a new team, one of my teammates asked, "Are you really playing with no shoes?" Word had gotten out. This is how unusual it was. But, if it made logical sense, I had the confidence to try such ideas, and I believed that my open-mindedness had helped my horses over the years.

How did it go? For those two tournaments, I didn't have any falls—perhaps I was a little more cautious on tight turns. I could feel the few extra inches that it took my horses to slide to a stop (though I took consolation in the knowledge that this slippage was natural and actually beneficial toward injury prevention.) But I can be either superstitious or hypersensitive about what things can alter my confidence around matches (sometimes these two feel like the same thing), and even though I hadn't had any dangerous slips, and our teams did fine (we were about 500 percent for our win/loss ratio), I didn't win either of those two tournaments. So I went back to having my horses shod for tournament polo only.

Undoubtedly, more time barefoot has improved their feet immensely. **//**

her to release her girth. I got off her and asked the cowboy to do the same. Tequila took a big breath. I held the reins and she looked at me like, *What am I doing down here while you are up there*? Then she got to her feet, shook, and we led her back to the trailer to recuperate.

This incident prompted me to rethink girths. Up to that point we had used leather girths, and only Bento could physically manage to do them tight enough for his and Adam's peace of mind to prevent the saddle from slipping during a game chukker. But I had recently seen a Quarter Horse client who was using a neoprene cinch on her Western saddle. I found an English version—it had elastic on both sides—and although at first Bento and Adam were dubious of its safety, I eventually convinced them that the "stickiness" of the neoprene more than compensated for the lack of tightness in the hold. We've used these girths exclusively ever since,

/ **11.3** / Adam and I believe farriery is so important that we now most often do our own horses barefoot trimming ourselves, despite it being back-breaking work. Our favorite printed resource is *The Essential Hoof Book* by Susan Kauffman and Christina Cline (Trafalgar Square Books, 2017).

/ 11.4 / The barn aisle is where many decisions are made and many stories are told. Make it a place where the essentials are met.

and never had a problem with either saddle slippage or horses coming off the field unable to breathe.

There are two recent research papers very relevant to the horse industry. One shows that during maximal exercise the temperature in the tendon increases and that this increase in temperature puts the horse at increased risk for tendon injury. The second paper showed that placement of polo bandages increased the temperature of the leg. Taking these two together, horse people should be wary of wrapping legs needlessly. As I have said before, *have a reason for what you are doing.* If the reason is because those four white bandages make your horse "look so pretty" (I know they do!), then take them off. The use of polo wraps is to prevent lacerations. *Only.* They do not offer much protection

★ Horse Clothing

The pros of body clipping are that the horse is aesthetically more pleasing and is cleaner. In a hot climate, especially out of season (for example, when a horse makes a drastic change of latitude for competition), it is necessary. The cons are that the horse is more spirited, and it takes a lot of manpower to blanket well enough (which I define by changing the weight of the blanket throughout the day's 24-hour cycle to match the weather) to mimic the natural insulation of hair. And no matter how dutifully you change and dry and buy blankets, they will always be less perfect at protecting the horse from the vagaries of the weather than what nature provided. And think of all the hours of work one would save by not blanketing and fly-sheeting (how about putting that money and time into good stabling and turnout design?). I believe that there is some anthropomorphizing going on in the human brain when we think about wanting to "clothe" our horses! A heavy, confining blanket is probably not what most horses want to wear. Consider the issue from the horse's perspective—as Adam mentioned earlier, the horse's *umwelt*—and see where that takes you. //

from blunt trauma. They do not offer much support. They are very effective at what they are meant to do—prevent another horse's hoof from gouging a cut into the area.

With this recent information I told our groom to please leave the wraps in place for as short a time as possible and only use them during game situations. This is such a good example of not only how "more is not better" but also how human "innovations" can actually create iatrogenic (human-caused) harm.

// Winning Point

Putting proper emphasis on horse care decisions is like learning your ABCs—it is the foundation of everything else that happens. This is the classic case where although things are simple—feed good forage and find a good farrier—they are not always easy to accomplish. Hopefully this information helps you properly prioritize what your horse really needs, which will then provide a healthy basis for all else to blossom. //

★ Lower Your Cross-Ties

Many cross-ties in barns I visit are attached so high on the walls that horses are forced to extend their necks while tied. Heights of the rings should be adjusted so that a horse's nose can be level with the point of his shoulder. In humans, studies have shown that posture affects mood. Head carriage is an important aspect to observe in a horse—we all know intuitively that a relaxed horse lowers his head. So maybe, like in the human, we can facilitate a proper posture (lowered head/flexed neck) to encourage a desirable mood (relaxed).

Tip: If you are in a barn where the cross-ties are high, clip them to the upper halter rings by the horse's jaw rather than the ones at the nose. //

end *of* chapter 11

A.S.

CHAPTER

12

Travels with Horses

Life is one damn thing after another.

– Mark Twain –

// Travels with Horses

CHAPTER 12

The miles that our horses logged during the busiest decade of my career (basically 1997 to 2007) were impressive. This travel was necessary for getting to tournament venues, but the inherent risks were great. For ten summers, we hauled my best string of 9 to 12 ponies from our farm in Aiken, South Carolina, to Santa Barbara, California, and back again. Assuming all went well, that was five, 8- to 12-hour days in each direction, with overnights in some pretty basic facilities. Plus, each winter my string shipped to Wellington, Florida—a ten-hour haul with no hiccups. For the summers I wasn't in California, we were on the road for the northeastern 20-goal circuit in Greenwich, Connecticut; Hamilton, Massachusetts; and Saratoga or Bridgehampton, New York.

These ponies notched frequent-flyer miles, too. Nine flew roundtrip to England for the 1999 summer season (see chapter 6—p. 88). And seven went roundtrip Miami to Buenos Aires for the 2004 Argentine Open. In 2001, three of them took a domestic flight one-way LAX to JFK, in order to make the first match of the USPA Gold Cup immediately after playing the Pacific Coast Open finals on the West Coast. Additionally, there were two summers in Wyoming; two Silver Cups in Norman, Oklahoma; a fall season in Houston, Texas; and regular week-long trips to Columbus, Georgia, and Pt. Clear, Alabama, for the southeastern 16-goal circuit most falls. Basically, we were going everywhere. If initially my motto had been, *Have mallets, will travel*, later it became, *Have mallets* ***and*** *horses, will travel.*

For most of these trips, I worried about my horses while they were on the road, but I knew Shelley had taken care of their stress-reduction needs as best she could, and I viewed travel as a necessary step to play tournament polo. It is only more recently, with fewer playing commitments and a strengthened connection to a group of homebreds we raised since Day One, that I view long travel with more concern and reflection. The last long trip my horses made was for a summer season in Wyoming in 2021. Though I didn't drive them myself, I kept a journal of their days on the road. Here's my account of that trip.

Wednesday, June 30th, 7:30 am

"Caipirinha, Rum Runner, Nuri, Vee, Bondi, Peace Train, Fanfare, Gossip, LolliBopp, Snapshot, BeBopp, Timote," Rel called out the loading order as she patrolled the barn aisle one last time before their imminent departure for Big Horn, Wyoming.

The Cummins diesel engine droned at the front of the gooseneck, warming for the 2000-mile journey that lay ahead. Hopefully, our 7:30 am start was late enough to miss the Atlanta traffic. I handed Scott each of my horses in turn, and he led them up the ramp of the aluminum trailer, tied them facing left "just loose enough," and swung their partitions closed.

"Easy there, girl, it's okay. There you go, your friend's right beside you," Scott cooed as he loaded.

In addition to being an expert professional driver, he was also a horseperson who cared about the individuals that made up his precious cargo.

"That brown one has a head like Bag Lady," he commented.

I realized that some of these ponies were the sons and daughters of horses he had hauled for me "back in the day." We'd both been doing this for quite a while.

"That's because he's her son," I responded.

It was my groom, Rel, who had itemized the trailer's contents—buckets, bandages, blankets, wheelbarrows, pitchforks, shovels, hoses, tack, feed, bandages, medications, timothy and alfalfa bales—and then packed it tight. As we stood there in the morning mist, the rig appeared to be brimming: hay bales snubbed to the flatbed, spare tires bolted behind the cab and under the gooseneck. On his second or third try, Timote grudgingly climbed on-board—he didn't like being in the caboose—and we were loaded. The hanging doors were swung closed and bolted, the ramp hoisted up, and they were off!

Scott inched the rig down the driveway and out onto Langdon Road. Rel followed several hundred yards back in her own vehicle, with her faithful dog, Tripp, riding shotgun. *Please let this trip be a smooth one*, I thought.

At 7:43 pm Rel texted: *Made it to Kentucky! Had one blowout on the trailer but Scott got it changed no problem* (💪). A quarter of the outbound trip was complete, but the blowout was a cause for concern.

Thursday afternoon I phoned Rel. I was already second-guessing my decision to send 12 horses. More than second-guessing, I had concluded that I was an idiot for making it. What was that definition of insanity? Repeating the same mistake and expecting a different result. That was me. Every time we had hauled 12 in the past, things always went wrong. *What had I been thinking?*

"We've had two more blowouts on the same, rear right trailer tire, and we're waiting at a truck stop somewhere in Missouri," Rel said.

"You mean we're out of spares?"

Of course, they wouldn't have had time to repair yesterday's blown tire, after arriving at their layover spot in Kentucky. And who could have imagined three blowouts in two days. And they were only halfway into Day Two's trip! To make matters worse, one of the truck tires was losing air, they suspected from a leaky valve, so Scott was waiting for the mechanic to check the valve stems, and hopefully repair or replace the blown trailer tires. And the truck stop was busy.

It sounded like a full-blown disaster in progress. All I could think about was thirsty horses waiting at a gas station... and that it was *my* fault. I was greedy, this is what it came down to. I had had a perfectly good group of 9 horses to bring to Wyoming, but then I couldn't say no to taking one more (Snapshot) at the last minute. She had practiced so well two days before the trip. And I thought I might want to buy her and having a month to try her and enter her in her first tournament polo "my way" sounded ideal. But then... *Ugh. What was I doing at age 57 even thinking about buying more horses? And being greedy to have more good ones to take to Wyoming, as if this season was the be-all-and-end-all.*

I will never learn.

Even in the midst of a potential crisis, Rel still sounded calm and upbeat. "The good thing is it's cool today, so the horses are comfortable while we wait."

I imagined the horses standing in their narrow slots, waiting on the tarmac for God knows how long, already six to eight hours on the trailer. *Please let them be all right!* These were the times I resorted to prayer. I felt grateful that it was Scott and Rel there with our horses, and tried to accept that, even if I was largely to blame, the present situation was out of my control. I checked my phone every 10 minutes for the next several hours. Finally, I couldn't wait any longer, and at 7:03 pm I texted Rel:

Are you guys okay?

Yes! she responded. *Sorry I forgot to tell you we arrived! We got three spares for the trailer and had to get two stem valves changed on two truck tires.*

Yikes. Glad you could get it all done. Are the horses okay? Sounds like a long day. I'm sorry for taking 12. I should have learned my lesson by now. Good luck tomorrow!

Horses are okay. Tired but okay. This is a really nice overnight so they should be able to rest well.

Still positive.

Two smooth days later, early afternoon of the third of July, Rel texted:

Pulling into Big Horn now (😀😀).

Prepare for the worst, and hope for the best. I guess that's what it comes down to. I thought I had prepared adequately, but when stuff began to go wrong, and tires started "popping like Chiclets," I kept thinking of all the "coulda-woulda-shouldas." I did take the truck for a "trip check" with mechanics I trusted, but they'd missed the valve stems. And I should have taken the whole rig into my favorite Aiken discount tire store and had them look over every single trailer tire. And then I should have specifically asked Scott what "psi" he wanted the tires inflated to. But the main thing was taking 12 horses and the extra weight that added. Just like me—*wanting to have my cake and eat it too*. Lesson (finally) learned.

> ”
>
> When you're stuck in the storm, pray for luck, and make the best of it.
>
> MATTHEW MCCONAUGHEY, *GREENLIGHTS* (CROWN, 2020)

July 12th

It had been a little over a week since the horses arrived to their summer home at the Flying-H stable in Big Horn, Wyoming. It was a rough trip, especially with the bad day, and most had lost some weight. And they needed to get used to a new place—prairie brome pastures; irrigation ditches funneling snowmelt; hundreds of other polo ponies stabled in their vicinity; and mountain foothills, dotted with pronghorn antelope and mule deer, rising from the edge of the exercise track. It was a different environment.

But my best horse, Nuri, still seemed anxious. He was 11 and had traveled to plenty of away seasons, so he was already an experienced traveler. He was playing

★ Go with the Pro

The times I drive my own rig—usually down or back from Florida, or occasionally a two-day trip to or from New York or Massachusetts—I pretty much white-knuckle it, checking the tires constantly in my side-view mirrors. I usually can't sleep the night before a trip, so when I'm alone, I'll just get myself up—it could be midnight, one or two in the morning—catch the horses and go. Better to be driving, doing it, than tossing and turning in bed, worrying about whether I'll be able to get the lug nuts off if I have to change a spare. But the truth is that I trust an experienced, professional driver more than myself. And that's why we hired Scott. //

well, but Rel felt he had "something going on." He was staring fitfully at all the new sights, walked circles in his stall, and showed far less interest in his food than normal.

I called a veterinarian friend, Dr. Paul Wollenman. He was recently inducted into the Polo Hall of Fame for his veterinary prowess and is one of the very best. (Shelley teched for him before starting veterinary school, and still considers him a mentor, and in her words, "Probably the smartest person I know.")

Paul arriveed within hours that same morning and asked me to lead Nuri out of his stall and onto the grass, where he observed his disinterested grazing for a minute, and announced: "Let's tube him with some charcoal. He probably developed a stomach ulcer on the trip, and this will help him." He also prescribed a half a tube of Gastrogard® once a day for the next three days. Within hours, Nuri was acting more like his confident self.

August 3rd

The older I got, the more disruptive long trips felt. The mothers of the homebreds I played had logged tens of thousands of travel miles. And I never used to worry about the hardship of the travel until we lost a talented young mare, Powder River, to *pleurisy* (inflammation of the pleural membrane that lines the chest wall and covers the lungs) after a terrible trip from Aiken to Florida. I had sent her with a trainer on their rig, and some 16 hours after departing our farm, they finally limped into Lake Worth, Florida. The mare developed the infection in the lining of her lungs, and five days later she was dead. Horses are generally resilient, and often recuperate unscathed from a rough trip, but that tragedy caused me to never again take my horses trips for granted.

When we were breeding horses, necessarily we sold the odd horse. And the offspring from certain mares seemed to sell themselves. One year we sold a late two-year-old named ShBopp. She was Hale Bopp's first foal. She had just been started under saddle, and while I had taught her to load, the farthest she'd ever driven in a trailer was about a mile down the road. The deal with the buyer was that we'd organize her transport to their facility in Wellington, Florida. It was extremely sad to see her go, but the offer was something we couldn't refuse. Still, the question remained as to how to get her down there safely. It was Shelley who came up with the plan:

"Scott can drive my two-horse down and back, and we'll send Mas O Menos with ShBopp for company. Mas O can spend a night down there, and Scott will drive her home the next day."

It was a perfect plan, so perfect that we used the same formula several years later when one of ShBopp's younger sisters, BoppBopp, made the same trip. Mas O Menos was a retired polo pony and eventer we utilized as a nanny, and she had been the foals' pasturemate and protector ever since they'd been weaned from their mother. Both trips went off without a hitch.

★ Mom and Nanny

When Hale Bopp got beyond her breeding years, she and Mas O Menos lived together in the same pasture and ate Equine Senior each morning out of adjacent ground bins. Now they are buried together under the same oak tree below our house. //

August 28th

It was my last game, and a finals at the Flying-H. It was raining, but they would try everything to play because it was the final weekend of the season. *I know how to play these games.* I hadn't won a tournament yet that summer, and it would be nice to go out with a "W." *But don't push, let it come. Do what makes me feel good out there, and enjoy.*

The horses would depart in two days. So much still to do. Preventive medicine was the ticket. I'd already had all the truck's valve stems checked. The brand inspection (a Wyoming state requirement) had been completed, and the Coggins and health certificates were in order. That morning I needed to check the truck and trailer tire pressures—now I knew I wanted them 10 to 20 psi below the specs because they would heat up so much on the road, and I knew what had happened last time! I'd depart in my car the next morning. Scott arrived by plane the following night. This way the horses had a day to rest, and then they'd leave Monday morning. Only 9 horses were traveling this time: Peace Train would be taken on consignment by another pro. BeBopp and Timote were returning with Brook Ledge direct to their owners in Boston. It was still gonna be a long trip, but it was less weight for everyone to carry—especially those four trailer tires!

August 30th, 3:58 pm

I received a text from Rel:

"Day 1 was very smooth! How is your trip going?"

Phew. Still many miles to go, but that was a great start.

"Just made it to Georgia. All good. Thanks, and good luck!"

I was making my own drive in two days, a little crazy, but I was dying to get home. Listening to books on tape, munching on the cooler full of snacks I had packed, camping roughly halfway at Weston Bend state park near Kansas City.

I made it to Aiken, driving my car basically the same route that Scott and Rel were travelling with the horses. It *was* a haul. Long, straight highway across the center of South Dakota, from Rapid City to Sioux Falls. It was beautiful open country, with the short-grass prairies in the western section of the state. I could picture the herds of bison that once roamed the space. And then, approaching the Missouri River from the west, it was more of everything—cars, trees, agriculture, gas stations. Then south and east, a slanted diagonal for several hundred miles. It was hard to know what state you were in through this section—South Dakota, Nebraska, Iowa, Kansas—as you shadowed the banks of the Missouri River, corn rows on all sides. (And that must have been soybeans? And possibly sun hemp with the yellow flowers?) Once you reached Kansas City, it was more or less due east toward St. Louis and the confluence of the Missouri and Mississippi rivers. After crossing the Mississippi, it felt strange to be in Illinois for a spell (maybe because it feels nothing like Chicago, and it was hard to imagine you were in the same state as that metropolis). But before you knew it, there appeared a Welcome to Kentucky sign. And that felt odd, too. Bluegrass and Thoroughbreds and tobacco barns, so close to the launching point of Lewis and Clark?

A

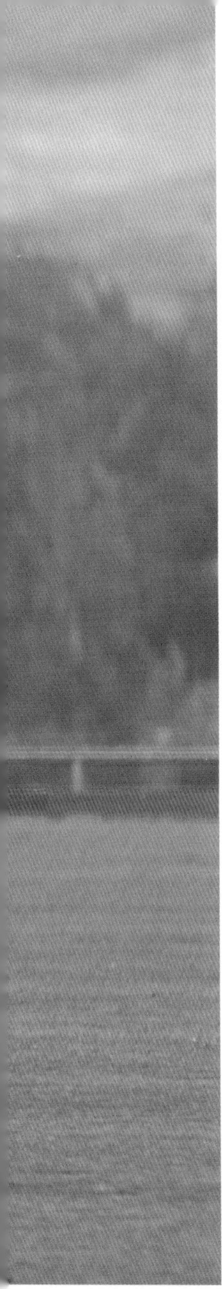

/ 12.1 A–G / Play-by-play photos of my fall with Vee. Going flat-out for goal. Neck shot. Whippy mallet. Hobbled. Going down in a heap. Aftermath. And…fortunate ending.

And then, as suddenly as it came, Kentucky, too, was gone. And the rolling green hills welcomed you with something familiar. The first sign of Appalachia—once the "Cherokee Nation." Kudzu and Bermuda grass and longleaf pines. Nashville, then Chattanooga, rain clouds uncorking a deluge—I figured it must be the hurricane I'd heard of on the news. It slowed highway traffic to 35 miles per hour. All vehicles' hazards were on, with drivers tight-fisted and focused as they sloshed through the clouds and water. This was the way I would be driving my rig—white-knuckles—even in fine weather. *I couldn't see shit!* Thank God for the assisted cruise control, keeping me safely back behind the brake lights of slowing cars I could not see.

And then appeared the first sign for *ATLANTA*, the storm petering, and I thought about all the soccer games that I drove my kids to in the surrounding suburbs. Then straight through downtown Atlanta, beautiful, and still, after the storm. It felt like home turf, even though I was still 200 miles away from home. But, *I got this!* And I upped it to 12 or even 15 miles per hour over the speed limit—not my usual 10. And the Audible book was good (*Underworld* by Don Dellilo)—*amazing*, really. And the miles ticked away on those tires that the Bridgestone people back in Sheridan, Wyoming, said were "good for one more trip, and then think about changing them."

And then I hit that dirt road, Langdon Road, our home road with just a slight washboard, and the cats were in the driveway. This was the route that my rig was traveling with its precious, tired cargo.

September 2nd

When we heard the trailer hit the washboard on Langdon Road, it was about 2:45 pm the next day. Scott always drove slowly in and out of our farm. I liked it—slow and steady, ease 'em on out and ease 'em on in. He felt the greatest risk of injury inside a trailer was at the beginning and end of each day's trip. They'd had four "smooth" days, the way it was supposed to be, and the horses had been on the rig less than eight hours today, coming from their overnight stop near Nashville, Tennessee. But when they smelled the farm, the horses kicked up a ruckus, and began banging and whinnying to be let out. I could imagine Caipirinha pawing her front feet, LolliBopp stomping her bandaged hinds against the wheel wells, and Rum Runner flaring her nostrils and trumpeting her desire to get off—*now!* They knew home. For four of them, it was the spot where they were born and raised.

Shelley and I rode our bicycles out as Scott backed expertly down the lane between the two pastures where the majority of the horses would be turned out. We were lucky for the cool weather; it was more like what they had come from in Wyoming. One group in each pasture: Nuri, Caipirinha, and Rum Runner in #7; Fanfare, Bondi, Gossip, Snapshot, and LolliBopp in #8 (they should be okay together, with no hind shoes and tired from the trip).

And last but not least, Vee unloaded and I hand-walked him across the polo field to his own pasture, up by the entrance to our farm. He's a pretty independent guy. And I was thankful that day that he remained calm, even while being led away from the rest of his trailer-mates. But he has to live alone. We've tried geldings and mares, tough ones and wimpy ones, young and old; but Vee invariably bares his teeth, sticks his tail and head up in the air, and turns into something like a fire-breathing dragon, bearing down on his prey with incredible force and ferocity. You can ride Vee in sets with other horses, graze him at liberty in front of the barn (like we'd done that summer at Flying-H, dropping several horses on the grass after sets while we untacked the ones we had ridden), and play him all-out through traffic on the polo field. But for some reason he will not tolerate other horses sharing a pasture with him. At age 15, it was hard to imagine he'd still do it, but it was not worth the risk. Plus, he'd earned his own paddock. Pasture #1 was "Vee's pasture." He'd won another BPP award that summer, bringing his tally to four. He also may have saved my life with how hard he tried to stay off of me in a wreck we'd had toward the end of August. I wrapped my mallet around his front legs on a neck shot—basically like throwing hobbles on in mid-stride—and we came down fast and hard. It surprised both of us. I had a moment to tuck a shoulder and roll.

Scott had a 5:00 am flight from Augusta in the morning (I would drive him). Rel needed, and deserved, some time off. There were a lot of odds and ends to manage: Nuri's bandage needed changing in the morning (speaking of a special horse); Gossip's stitches could come out over the next two to three days; the trailer needed to be unloaded and cleaned; countless loads of horse laundry of blankets and saddle pads needed to be washed. And I needed to remember to trim Bondi and Fanfare, who would remain turned out through the fall. In a few weeks, assuming all went according to plan, the other seven would play their next tournament game in Aiken. But now they would get eight full days of "R&R" on fresh pastures—enough time to relax and be horses for a spell, and hopefully regain any weight they may have lost on the trip. I was grateful that they'd made it safely back home. I figured maybe I should give thanks now, and not just pray when things looked bleak?

Thank you for helping them all make it back to the farm in one piece.

Stuff Still Happened

Over the years of shipping horses, we tried to take every precaution we could think of—allowing an extra day on longer trips, hiring experienced drivers, giving the horses immune boosters like echinacea pre-trip, and of course standing them beside their buddies—but stuff still happened. While being quarantined in wire corrals outside Ezieza Airport in Buenos Aires, Argentina, Duet ripped open her lower leg, requiring heavy antibiotics and a skin-graft. She missed the first part of the season that she had flown for, and the accident nearly ended her career. Powder

River, who I told you about earlier, had to be put down when she developed pleurisy after a 16-hour trailer ride. And an impaction that Beach Bum must have already sustained was compounded by a six-hour haul back from Columbus, Georgia, after her very first tournament. The colic became severe over the next 24 hours. She was taken to the University of Georgia equine hospital and operated on, but she died. The summer of 2018, Ming (a lovely black Chilean gelding) arrived in Santa Barbara with a pattern of parallel claw marks covering his back. The owner of the layover spot in New Mexico speculated that a bobcat must have jumped down on him from the barn rafters at night. (Rel thought he'd battled a mountain lion to keep it away from his mares. Only Ming knows what really happened!) And then there were several horses—Rum Runner, Dionysus, and Southern Class—for whom the stress of a long haul caused symptoms of EPM. In Dionysus's case, the first time I realized that something was wrong was when I jumped horse-to-horse onto him as a spare for a high-goal exhibition in Wyoming, and next thing I knew all four of his feet shot out from under him and he was lying sternal on the ground. My own feet, still in their stirrups, were resting on the grass. I think I was still considering what had just happened when he scrambled to his feet, and there was nothing else to do but gallop out on the field and finish the chukker.

// Winning Point

> Travel is a calculated risk that most equestrians accept in order to compete. If I hadn't been willing to ship (or fly) my horses to tournaments, then I couldn't have played polo professionally. And it follows that we wouldn't have owned, played, or maintained the amazing group of animals that we describe in these pages. There is a balance competitors strike between knowingly putting their horses at some risk, while still being conscientious stewards of their welfare. In the case of travel, as well as almost every aspect of horse management, it is our obligation as owners to minimize these risks to the best of our ability. Prepare to the teeth, and pray for safe travels. //

end *of* chapter 12

CHAPTER

13

Horse Stories

Be the person your horse wants you to be.

// Horse Stories

CHAPTER

13

In a myriad of ways, horses bring out the best in humans. Here are examples, from my experiences as a veterinarian, rider, and trainer, of how three horses enriched my life.

Gossip

Undoubtedly horses have made me, as they have made many before me and will affect many in the future, a better person. One recent memory involves arriving at an appointment to recheck a patient. The barn was empty, clean, and orderly when I walked in. One of the dogs who lived here was a little intimidating—he always growled at me—but he was nowhere in sight (I was generally more wary of the dogs than the horses). As I was doing a recheck on Gossip, a gelding I knew, I went ahead and caught him and led him into the barn. Just as I was getting my acupuncture needles out of my pouch, I heard my client and some neighbors call out, “Need any help?” as they walked on the path toward the barn from the house. I fatefully responded,

/ 13.1 / Fun over fences. Chester and me on the stadium jumping course at Stable View's Oktoberfest in Aiken, South Carolina.

”

Getting on a favorite horse is like slipping into the comfiest pair of sweatpants you own.

"I am good, no worries!" but just seconds later, the horse I had treated without any ado many times over the years decided that either he'd had enough or I was distracted and this was his moment, and whirled and kicked me squarely in the thigh. My client had rounded the corner of the barn in time to witness the whole debacle and came rushing toward me, asking if I was okay. I was lucky Gossip had no shoes (my client kept her horse barefoot), and I sensed my leg wasn't broken, but it sure hurt.

It certainly was not the first time I had felt like a fool, but perhaps professionally the worst. I tried my best to brush it off (and not to cry), and gladly accepted help to have someone else hold Gossip while I reinserted needles and attached the electroacupuncture machine. I was somewhat sheepish during the 20 minutes of

★ The Importance of Attention

I have spent a lot of time in my career taking the time to assess horses' personalities, calm them with massage, and use acupuncture techniques of sedating points to ground a horse before I may put in a needle that would *zing*. In this instance my lack of attention caught me out. I feel fortunate it is the only time it has happened. //

therapy, and the owner was so apologetic and wanted to bring me ice, which I initially politely refused. But after I extracted the needles and checked to make sure my patient's pain was gone, I relented, and I sat down in a comfy chair in the barn aisle with an ice pack on my leg, checking my watch surreptitiously to calculate the arrival time of my next appointment. The neighbors left, and the owner and I relaxed into an easy chat, talking about her horses and podcasts we'd listened to, all in the context of how she was grappling with a diagnosis of early-onset dementia. The overhead fan whirred, and I felt the pain and nerves ease away. It turned out that was the last time I ever saw my friend. In retrospect, I was so grateful to Gossip for kicking some sense into me—he made me slow down, sit down, and pay attention to a friend in need.

Chester K

Thank goodness the fence held. I had been on a nice trail ride with a friend and neighbor and was ambling back home along a dirt road with my horse Chester nicely relaxed and a little bit tired after almost two hours in the saddle. We were almost to the highway crossing, on the other side of which was home. I first noticed the steer about 100 yards away suddenly pick up his head from grazing, then fix his eyes in

/ **13.2** / Sky Blue, on the left, in true form. She is my special one.

our direction. I thought, *Certainly not,* but my cow sense I guess is not as developed as my horse sense because indeed, it *certainly was.*

Happening, that is: 1,000 pounds of steer first trotting then galloping—in that discombobulated, looking like they have three legs, running way—straight at us. There was only a horse wire fence between us, nowhere else to go, and one way home. Chester realized what was happening a few seconds after I did so I had time to gather my reins in one hand and hold the cantle of the saddle in the other. He spooked and bolted sideways, but I hung on, and then he responded to my aids (*Thank God*!) to stop and face the menace, who after reaching the fence and giving us a nasty look, dutifully trotted back to his herd. I could feel Chester's heart beating between my legs; he could probably feel mine pounding as well. We had survived together, I thought, as I eased him onward, talking to him reassuringly and effusively telling him what a good boy he was, despite my inward voice exclaiming, *I can't believe that just happened*! But as we continued along the road—remember, there was only one way home—the steer repeated the look, trot, gallop and charge two more times. Even as I write this it is still hard to believe it happened—we pranced and snorted and prayed until we were beyond that cow pasture. I know that if I didn't have such a long-term trusting relationship with Chester it wouldn't have ended well. I thank my lucky stars I was on him that day and we both made it out unscathed.

And the fence held.

Sky Blue

I have been fortunate to know many amazing horses. But a very special equine relationship for me started in 2009. Sky Blue was born on our farm on a sunny day in June. Her dam, Tequila, although a maiden mare, was a perfect mother, and Sky's months alongside her were blissfully (and rare in the breeding business) trouble-free.

When Sky was about five months of age we introduced my retired event mare Mas O (she had such a high social intelligence IQ that someone had once tried to buy her from me to "school" their young horses, and she successfully raised one foal of her own) into the pasture with Tequila, Sky Blue, and another mare and foal. I watched the new quintet carefully and the introduction went well. I would see Sky and her foal companion over the next month or two start spending more and more time with Mas O—at least when they were not running hell-bent for leather in the 10-acre pasture. I had it in my mind that I was going to try and start Sky Blue on my own, as a first-time endeavor, but I certainly had some second thoughts as I watched her zesty personality blossom!

When we eventually moved the two dams out of the pasture several months later, there was almost no drama. I don't do drama well. And the plan worked: after about five minutes of calling, the two foals just went to where Mas O was calmly grazing and hung out by her, perhaps a little closer for a few days, but otherwise fine. The mares, who had been pushing the foals off of nursing for a few weeks, remained agitated a little longer, but in a few hours were happily regrouped with the friends they hadn't seen in a while. I believe weaning is one of the single most consequential events in determining a horse's personality—for better or for worse—and I was determined to make decisions on our farm to lean toward the "for better."

So far so good.

When I began my training with Sky as a yearling, I wrote down three things I wanted to teach her:

/ **1** / Respect my space.

/ **2** / Follow a soft lead.

/ **3** / Yield to soft pressure.

It turned out that those precepts would be what I followed for the rest of my life with horses—they are now second nature. Nothing like some pressure to succeed added to a wee bit of danger to make one really think things through! I also realized with Sky that just in the act of haltering a horse in a paddock and then leading him through a gate, you were testing, practicing, and reinforcing each of the three goals (or not). *Every moment is a teaching moment.*

Sky as a two-year-old was a formidable thing to behold. I can't count how many times I watched her high-octane frolics in the field and thought, *How will I ride that?* But I simply committed to taking it one step at a time and told myself there was no time constraint and I could always get assistance if needed. As it turned out, she was easy. It helped that the way I was taught was to "do everything" on the ground first—I had an extensive pre-ride list. And eventually Sky checked all the boxes: was never rude or pushy; loved to follow me around and see what the next play session consisted of; moved all her body parts away from pressure. I worked tirelessly on myself and my cuing—ensuring that it was consistent so that when I did eventually step astride, she would still understand me. Day after day, I ended the session and silently repeated to myself, *I think I can ride that.*

We never had a bad moment together as a mounted pair. From the get-go, Sky was accepting of everything I asked her. She became a star polo pony, and her only fault was that she got super excited if horses ran a fence line when you were riding her—a remnant of when we had a stallion on the farm who would antagonize the mares in this way with his trumpeting. She loves our round pen to this day, and she would still be my favorite to show off on if I ever wanted to demonstrate to someone how a polo pony can move! Seeing her soft doe-eyes in our barn still melts my heart. And I like to believe that my caresses remind her she is my special one.

// Winning Point

Why are we so drawn to animals? I believe I touched on the answer in our first book, *Polo Life*:

> *Horses are beguiling because they demand—for safety, of necessity—that we pay close attention to them. They foster a state of mind, which in and of itself is one toward which humans gravitate. To paraphrase psychologist Mihaly Csikszentmihhalyi in his acclaimed book* Finding Flow *(Basic Books, 1998), "flow" experiences are characterized by high-skill and high-challenge demands, as well as having clear goals and feedback. He argues that the human brain is wired to perform its best under these situations, as well as find serenity. With horses being the intelligent and adaptive creatures they are, every session with them meets these criteria. There is a constant, live-wire connection between horse and rider, joining the two lives.* //

end *of* chapter 13

CHAPTER

14

Best or Favorite?

Your best horse is the one you play the best on.

– Alberto Pedro Heguy, DVM –

// Best or Favorite?

Writing these pages, I find myself sometimes distinguishing between a *favorite* horse and a *best* horse. This separation seems counterintuitive—wouldn't they be one and the same? But, in fact, it is not.

Recently someone asked me to name the best horses I had ever played. This was easy. Though I have competed scores of world-class ponies, there are three that were truly different: Pumbaa would be my first choice to play in a sudden-death chukka for my life. Amy was the most *complete* mare I had ever played. And Hale Bopp was my *favorite*.

Hale Bopp had many, many games when she was my best horse. And she had longevity on her side, too. I bought her at age six and played her until I was forced to retire her at age 17, and she hardly missed a game during this period. I credit her with helping me win more matches than any other horse. In her prime—it was a long *prime* of over a decade—I'd usually play her in the fourth and, if we were tied at the end of six, I'd start back on her in overtime. She was a game-changer for me, a game *winner*.

CHAPTER 14

/ 14.1 / Hale Bopp in flight form. She was a dream to play—think it, and we were doing it. (She always "hunkered-down" and pinned her ears back to run, and the red numbered saddle pad, used to select BPP prizes, indicates that this game was a tournament finals.)

And she accumulated six BPP prizes during her career to prove it: All of these were in high-goal tournaments at the 20-, 22-, and 26-goal levels.

How did she play? She stopped on a dime and stayed flat so that you could always get back to the ball. She had a burst of speed, turned like a top, and was quick-quick in the short play. *Think it* and we were *doing it*—that is how she played. So this explains why I consider her one of the *best* three horses I've ever played.

But why was she my *favorite*?

There is definitely an emotional element to *favoritism*. As for Hale Bopp, perhaps it had to do with how she came to me, or her appearance, or the heart she exhibited every time she entered the playing field. But, for whatever reason, I developed a connection with this little spark plug that survived well beyond her playing career.

She came in March of 1998, when I received a call from Roger Redman, someone I didn't know at the time, asking if I would like to try his horses.

"Of course," was my reply. In those days I would try anything. The seller was halfway into his trip, hauling six horses across the state of Florida.

We met the next morning at the Orchard Hill polo facility in Wellington. I found six nice-looking thoroughbreds tied to his trailer. They had varying degrees of polo experience, but most had played some low-goal tournament polo. "Be Bopp" was the name of a stout little black mare. Roger thought she was too small to play high-goal polo but asked if I wanted to sit on her in case I "knew anyone looking for a small horse, maybe a woman sponsor?"

Over the years I've joked with peers about trying prospects: If someone tells you they've got a "high-goal pony," run! But if a seller describes a "fun, easy horse," but they're not sure about the speed—be sure to try that one! Be Bopp looked just shy of 15 hands, certainly smaller than anything in my barn, but under saddle she felt wide and catty...and I asked if I could try her in a 26-goal practice game.

/ 14.2 A & B / Hale Bopp after retirement with her filly, BoppBopp.

I remember we played that same afternoon at Everglades, and she was even more impressive on the practice field. It felt like she could read and write out there. And it's always nice when another set of eyes confirms what you think you feel. In this case it was a friend and teammate, Roberto Gonzalez: "Adam, if you don't buy that mare, I will!"

He wasn't joking. I already knew that she *felt* amazing; now I knew she *looked* amazing, too. So I bought her. This was the period when the comet named Hale Bopp was visible on clear nights. And I thought it was serendipitous that Be Bopp had come to me at the same time that Hale Bopp adorned the night sky. So, once the logistics of a pre-purchase exam and payment were out of the way, I brought her to my barn and named her after that comet. After all, I was only changing one syllable of her former name, so I hoped that this would avoid any bad luck associated with the name-change-curse.

The next day my friend Mike Morton (who was visiting from Wyoming) walked down my barn aisle, peered in the stall at the new mare, and reported, in his distinctive drawl: "I hate to be the one to tell you this, Adam, but this mare's too small for you."

Two days later I took Hale Bopp to the field for a 26-goal game against Outback, played her a couple minutes as a spare in the first half, and ended up finishing the last half of the sixth on her in a nail-biter that we won by one or two goals. And the mare went from strength to strength, soaring on the playing field for the next 11 years, like the comet she was named after.

Though pure Thoroughbred, her appearance was of a shiny Quarter Horse nugget—short-coupled, dark brown (black, really, but the Jockey Club papers registered her color as "dark brown") with a huge shoulder, a big ass, and a strip and snip. Her ears curved in like two crescent moons, almost to the point of touching. And when she stretched her head down to run, or got competitive in a ride-off, her ears laid back flat. She would go into any bump—she could care less about the size of the other horse—and most of these she won. But her exceptional quality was her ability to decelerate quickly, effortlessly...and then she could spin and scoot off again in another direction. I have memories of (and recently watched a video of this in the Gold Cup Finals) an opponent bringing the ball behind us on a knock-in, and together she'd check, turn, and accelerate, so smooth that it felt like one motion, to meet the hitter and steal the ball from a surprised opponent. Usually these recoveries resulted in goals for our team, since we had just stolen the ball from their last player back.

Hale Bopp loved to be groomed and brushed and relished a good back-scratching. And 11-some years after I received Roger's out-of-the-blue call, Hale Bopp's playing career ended, and she retired on our farm. She foaled four beautiful babies over the remaining 11 years of her lifespan. And now she is buried under a live oak on the edge of a field below our house. I remember during her years of retirement, when it was my turn to check the horses, Hale Bopp would position her body along the fence for rubbing, and I always scratched her back just a little bit longer than any of the others.

My favorite.

// Winning Point

Shelley and I have developed special bonds with so many of our horses that I almost feel guilty calling Hale Bopp my favorite. But it's the truth. And it turns out we're not the only ones who appreciated her presence and accomplishments on the field. I was recently notified by the nominating committee that Hale Bopp is to be publicly recognized as a "Horse to Remember" through her 2023 induction into the Polo Hall of Fame in Lake Worth, Florida. She earned it. //

end *of* chapter 14

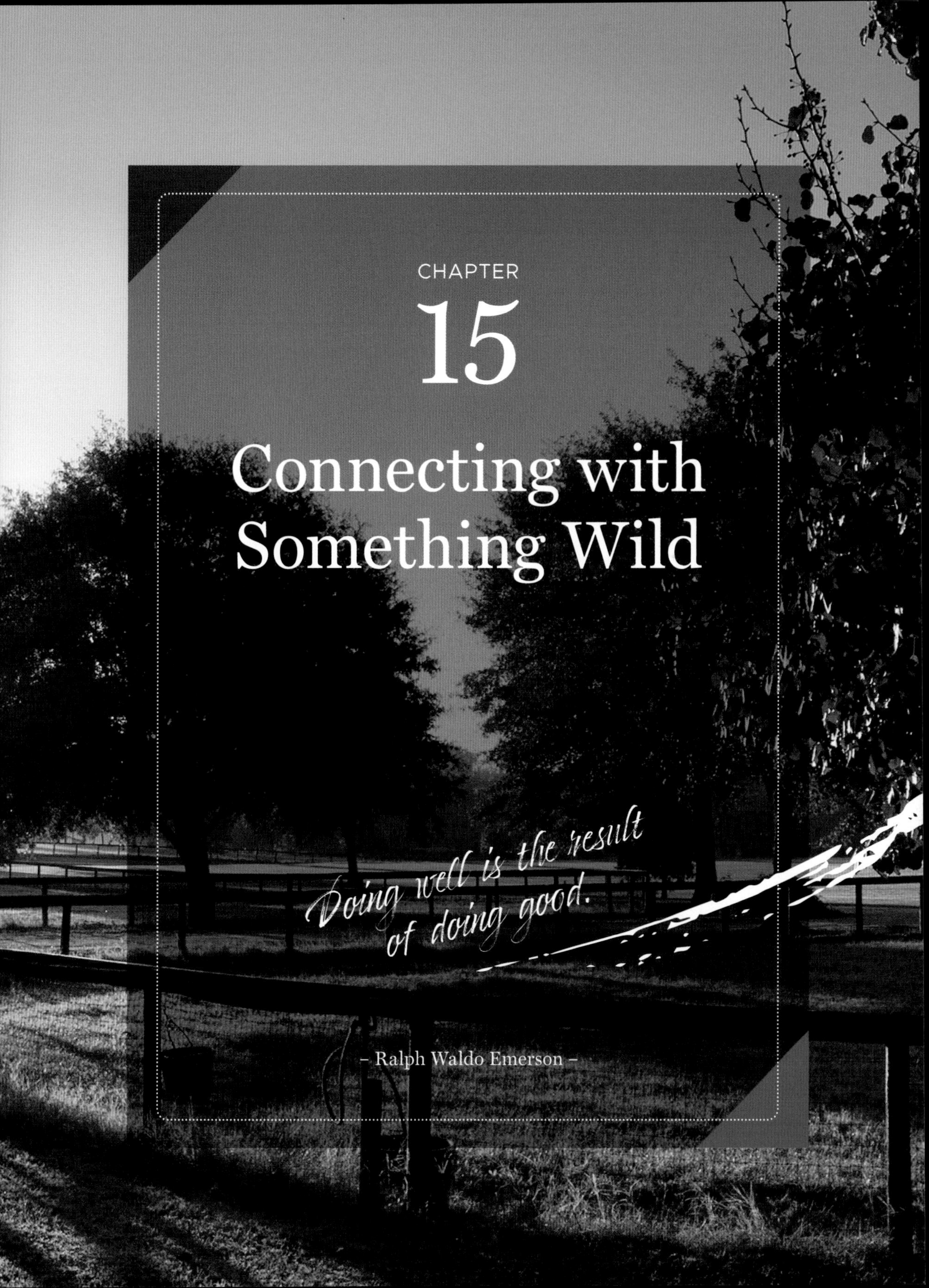

CHAPTER

15

Connecting with Something Wild

Doing well is the result of doing good.

– Ralph Waldo Emerson –

// Connecting with Something Wild

CHAPTER

15

Rewilding is a concept we have been applying to areas of our farm (which is mostly in a conservation easement). In practice for us, it means to allow the natural state of flora and fauna to recover and take over—we live in peace with the beavers to allow good water flow, plant long-leaf pines to restore the native forest, and apply regenerative agriculture methods to "fertilize" our fields. The concept is also relevant to horses.

The way many horses must live is not consistent with their true nature. *They* need to be rewilded. Horses need space and social interaction; if put in stalls 24 hours a day, 365 days a year, their health will deteriorate, both mentally and physically. German Olympian Ingrid Klimke makes a bold statement in her book *Training Horses the Ingrid Klimke Way*: "If I couldn't turn them out freely, I would not want to keep horses anymore."

And for humans? Certainly—*nature deficit disorder* is real. One of the biggest gifts horses give us is a connection to nature, to something wild.

The relationship between horses, people, and open space is interdependent: horses need open space to be their best; open space needs humans to protect it; and humans need horses to remind us we are part of the earth.

We may use horses for all sorts of different purposes—we have been breeding them for millennia to do disparate jobs—and we are presuming that domesticity is a given. But greater awareness of horse welfare and needs—*without anthropomorphizing*—is required if horse sports are to continue. Competing with horses is a privilege, and also a serious responsibility. The pressure we apply in order to get our horses to perform a task—clearing fences, cutting cows, playing polo, executing flying changes, sliding to a halt, racing, chasing, pacing—to their full potential must be thoughtful and nuanced. And the release from this pressure should be readily apparent to our equestrian partners. It is our responsibility to care for them in such a way that they can flourish. We must act upon our values.

Paying attention to horses' deep-seated needs is what allows for harmony and freedom. It isn't easy! Working daily with horses is indeed a labor of love—at times it may feel like our efforts go unrewarded. But practice and patience are requirements for developing the level of communication needed to achieve

our goals in partnership with such a spirited animal as a horse. When legendary cellist Pablo Casals was asked why he continued to practice for three hours a day at the age of 93, he replied, "Because I believe I'm making progress." That's a worthy goal at any age and at any stage—*keep making progress.*

In the process of writing this book together, it became clear to us that we each have our limitations, and that it is only in the joining of our strengths that we attained anything close to providing the complete package for our horses. There can be an inherent tension between the competitor and the caretaker, between the one who wants to ask everything from the horse and the one who is trying to keep the horse in one piece back at the barn. A die-hard competitor sometimes needs to lean on a trainer, a veterinarian, or a trusted groom to help him make good horsemanship decisions. A team like this will come to the realization that the possibility for a win/win does, in fact, exist. For, if there is anything we have sought to demonstrate in these pages, it is that doing good for your horse will rebound for you not only as a competitor but also as a person. We owe it to ourselves, as well as to our horses, to strive to be better. //

// Acknowledgments

Acknowledgments

A huge thanks is due to Robb Scharetg, who graciously offered his expertise and time to capture us on film with our horses on New Haven Farm. We are so appreciative of your talent and generosity. Also, thank you to Kate Meiczkowska who, after contributing her drawings to our first book *Polo Life: Horses, Sport, 10 and Zen*, allowed us to repurpose them. Her line drawings add beautiful artistic flair to *Winning with Horses*.

Shelley Schmidt ably converted a hodgepodge of prints to proper digital format, thus allowing us to make our deadline! Although we don't particularly like looking at the photographs of Vee's fall, many thanks to Kalie Roos for capturing it on film, and allowing us to use the images. And to our dear friend David Lominska—we appreciate your dedication to filming polo over the decades and capturing so many moments. The memories are treasured.

We are so grateful to Rebecca Didier for her belief in our project and her support at every step of the way. To all at Trafalgar Square Books: thank you for your dedication to improving the welfare of the horse. //

// Index

Page numbers in *italics* indicate illustrations.

Index